A
RETREAT
with
the
PSALMS

A Retreat
with the Psalms

*Resources for Personal
and Communal Prayer*

John C. Endres and Elizabeth Liebert

● PAULIST PRESS ● New York/Mahwah, N.J.

COVER DESIGN ● LYNN ELSE

TYPE DESIGN ● CASA PETTA

Library of Congress Cataloging-in-Publication Data

Endres, John C., 1946-
   A retreat with the Psalms : resources for personal and communal prayer / John C. Endres and Elizabeth Liebert.
      p. cm.
   Includes bibliographical references.
   ISBN 0-8091-4026-8 (alk. paper)
   1. Bible. O.T. Psalms—Criticism, interpretation, etc. 2. Prayer—Biblical teaching. I. Liebert, Elizabeth, 1944- II. Title.

BS1430.6.P68 E63 2001
223'.206—dc21

                                                                    2001021230

Published by Paulist Press
997 Macarthur Boulevard
Mahwah, New Jersey 07430

www.paulistpress.com

Printed and bound in the
United States of America

CONTENTS

Music Chart Abbreviations

G   *Gather: Comprehensive.* Chicago: GIA Publications, 1994.

G&P   *Glory and Praise.* Second Edition. Portland, Oreg.: OCP Publications, 1997.

HEC   *The Hymnal 1982: According to the Use of the Episcopal Church.* New York: Church Hymnal Corp., 1982.

LBW   *Lutheran Book of Worship.* Minneapolis, Minn.: Augsburg, 1982.

NCH   *New Century Hymnal.* Cleveland, Ohio: The Pilgrim Press, 1995.

PC   *The Psalter: Psalms and Canticles for Singing.* Louisville, Ky.: Westminster/John Knox, 1993.

PH   *Presbyterian Hymnal.* Louisville, Ky.: Westminster/John Knox, 1990.

UMH   *United Methodist Hymnal: Book of United Methodist Worship.* Nashville, Tenn.: United Methodist Publishing House, 1989.

W   *Worship: A Hymnal and Service Book for Roman Catholics.* Third Edition. Chicago: GIA Publications, 1986.

WOV   *With One Voice: A Lutheran Resource for Worship.* Minneapolis, Minn.: Augsburg, 1995.

Acknowledgments

If it takes a whole village to raise a child, it takes at least a neighborhood to produce a book. Our neighbors, from whom we have borrowed many figurative cups of flour and sugar, rides, and other favors, are wonderfully numerous and diverse.

Mary Rose Bumpus, R.S.M., our collaborator from the beginning as presenter, liturgist, musician, homilist, and choir director, knows this retreat inside out. Her work appears all through this book, but most overtly in the Morning Prayer and Evening Prayer services at the end of most chapters. The service on page 159 is based on one developed by Valerie Endter. Barbara Williams, S.N.J.M., originally posed the idea of a retreat based on the psalms, and the California Province of the Sisters of the Holy Names of Jesus and Mary provided us with our initial retreat support team. The staffs of Loyola Retreat House in Portland, Oregon, and Bon Secours Retreat House in Marriotsville, Maryland, also hosted psalms retreats in later years. Shorter retreats, conferences, and workshops allowed us the opportunity to expand and refine our work. Among others, these included: Westminster Presbyterian Church in Eugene, Oregon; Lafayette-Orinda Presbyterian Church in California; and the Institute of Spirituality and Worship at the Jesuit School of Theology at Berkeley. The "Psalms and Practice" conference, organized by Steven Reid at Austin Presbyterian Seminary in May 1999, provided rich ecumenical dialog on the "practice" of the psalms, which was precisely our subject.

Our gratitude goes to Martha Starret, O.P., whose transcribed talk, "*Lectio Divina* as Body Praise," appears in chapter 2. The experience and comments of many others is woven throughout these pages, especially of our students at the Jesuit School of Theology at Berkeley and San Francisco Theological Seminary, both in the Graduate Theological Union. We are grateful to George Griener, S.J., dean at JSTB, who provided funding for editing the manuscript from the faculty development fund.

Jo Milgrom and Maureena Fritz offered us their published materials and encouraged us to use them. Westminster/John Knox, Oregon Catholic Press, and GIA (Gregorian Institute of America) graciously sent us their recent psalm-based music for enrichment. Michelle Walker helped us to assemble and present the musical resources appearing in the chapters. Robert Kramish read the entire manuscript with a critical eye.

Each of us owes more than we can acknowledge to our respective religious communities—the Washington Province of the Sisters of the Holy Names of Jesus and Mary, and the Oregon Province of the Society of Jesus—and to our family members. We dedicate this labor of love to our parents, Irene and Joseph Liebert and Patricia and John Endres. May they rest in peace.

Thanks to each of you, named and unnamed, who composed the "neighborhood" in which this book was born.

Introduction

This book is designed to guide persons who wish to enter into deeper prayer based on the psalms. These ancient prayers have formed countless persons, Jews and Christians alike, over the centuries. In a time when psalms are no longer the daily bread of most believers, this book will help to reimagine, remember, and reconnect with the long and rich tradition of psalm prayer. Two simple assumptions ground this book: The psalms are a school of prayer. Their pedagogical role is as important today as at any time in their long history.

We will present different kinds, or genres, of psalms so that their variations clearly emerge. We do so for two reasons. First, the psalms originate in corporate worship settings. The more we can set up correspondences between these ancient worship settings and today's corporate prayer and worship, the easier it will be to reclaim the psalms for today's corporate prayer. Second, when people learn the full extent of psalm prayer, it frees them to become equally wide-ranging in their personal prayer. The psalms model great breadth of affects, metaphors, images, forms, and cadences, offering rich patterns for our prayer.

Furthermore, personal prayer and corporate worship are intimately intertwined. While community worship subtly teaches, models, and reinforces the prayer of individuals, the prayer experiences of those who gather enriches and enlivens corporate worship by asking it to reflect the full range of human-divine interaction. Knowing the psalm genres allows those responsible for planning worship to select more appropriate psalm settings; likewise, the full range of psalm genres can extend the range of corporate worship.

This work was born of our love for the psalms and our desire that others might also love and pray them. John Endres, S.J., teaches Old Testament at the Jesuit School of Theology in Berkeley. He regularly offers courses that unpack the psalms in their original setting as well as the history of their exegesis and use in Christian communities throughout history. Elizabeth Liebert, S.N.J.M., teaches spirituality at San Francisco Theological Seminary. She works with spirituality and spiritual guidance, developing praying communities and their leadership. Because we both regularly teach Roman Catholic, Anglican, and Protestant ministry students, we have sought to make this work accessible to all these traditions, especially through our examples.

We invite several groups of people to make themselves at home in this book and to employ it in different ways. First, those who want to deepen their psalm-based prayer can use these chapters and the prayer suggestions at their conclusion to form the basis of the personal prayer. One might spend a week, a month, or even longer with each genre, exploring various types of prayer with different psalms. Another might choose to employ one style of prayer, such as *lectio divina*, through several genres. Still another person might pick up the book at different seasons of life: in a period of grief, becoming immersed in lament psalms; in community tragedy, centering on communal laments; during great celebration, focusing on thanksgiving psalms; or during Holy Week, probing the penitential psalms. We encourage you to use what you find helpful.

Prayer or study groups can profitably anchor a seven-week study on the various psalm genres. Groups could be organized several ways. For example, one group might open with a psalm, spend some time commenting on what struck the members from their own study, share their experiences of praying the psalms during the preceding week, and close their time together by praying the common prayer provided in each chapter. In this model the group forms a kind of spiritual guidance and support community for its members as they pray the psalms in the context of their individual lives. Following a different model, a group could open with a few minutes of discussion on the psalm genre, then pray a psalm together using a group version of *lectio divina*, concluding with a few minutes of sharing about the movements and insights that arose during their shared prayer. Or they could agree to develop together a visual response around a selected psalm. A group that wishes to proceed at a more leisurely pace can linger for several sessions on a single genre, studying and praying different psalms, or praying in different ways with the same psalm, or any combination that suits its needs.

A lectionary study group could choose to highlight the psalms for Sunday worship. If the group includes clergy, they might choose to preach on the psalm text for a period of time. This book can help tailor the study of those planning worship; in addition, it may suggest psalm-based hymns that, together with the sermon, offer deeper psalm fare to the congregation. The psalms could significantly deepen their effect on the community's common prayer, their cadence creeping more into the language of individual and shared prayer.

Church groups can profitably use portions of this book for evening or weekend retreats. For example, one church retreat on Palm Sunday weekend began on Friday evening with a brief exposition on praying with the psalms and an introduction to *lectio divina* for personal prayer and concluded with community Night Prayer (Compline). The next day, the morning session focused on lament psalms and the afternoon session on thanksgiving psalms. The retreat closed with Evening Prayer. The next day, Palm Sunday, the sermon was based on the psalms that appear in the lectionary that day and throughout Holy Week. Another liturgical season might suggest different genres for a retreat focus. Once introduced to praying with the psalms, individuals can continue on their own with the help of this book.

In fact, this book was born from a retreat, and we imagine it continuing to ground individual and group retreats. For individuals who are able to take a few days for personal retreat, it provides an outline for prayer and can be used with or without the assistance of a spiritual guide. Depending on the length of the retreat, one or more genres can become the focus. An eight-day retreat might cover most of the genres. In the bibliography we indicate a few books most useful for personal retreat.

The first two chapters offer introductory material upon which the remainder of the book rests. Chapter 1 introduces biblical material: Hebrew poetry, psalm genres, and recommended translations and versions. Chapter 2 introduces various forms of prayer that will appear in the subsequent chapters. Chapters 3 through 8 treat the various psalm genres and show how a genre can be congenial and helpful to contemporary people when their life settings are similar. Each of these chapters contains an exposition of the genre followed by suggestions for personal and group prayer based on psalms of the genre. Chapter 9 focuses on appropriating the psalms in our lives. The final chapter addresses the role of Christ in psalm prayer.

Now we invite you to stop reading. This is not a text-book! Take some time to ask yourself how and when you wish to enter more deeply into the world of the psalms. Read over the table of contents—maybe one type of psalm matches your present situation and mood. Do you wish to begin with praise? gratitude? petition? Perhaps the Holy Spirit is inviting you to begin where your desires are. When you have set aside time and place, invite God into your reading, study, meditation, and prayer. The world of the psalms is large enough for all the ways we humans hear, study, see, and respond. The Book of Psalms will gradually lead us to explore new vistas in worship and prayer. We urge you to accept this invitation.

One
Entering the World of the Psalms

The collection of one hundred and fifty psalms combines an amazing variety of subjects, moods, attitudes, and even types of theology and spirituality. All share one thing in common: they are poetry. In earliest times, when psalmists composed and wrote them down, they probably sang or chanted these prayer poems. In this chapter we explore both the commonality and the variety in the Book of Psalms. We first explore Hebrew poetry, how it works, and how different it is from much poetry in the English language. Experiencing psalms as poetry allows us to pray with them in special ways. Next we explore the variety in the psalms, the different types of psalms that suit many different life situations. We remain indebted to the insights of biblical scholar Herman Gunkel, whose description of different literary forms in the Book of Psalms still informs much of our exposition of psalms. The quick overview of psalm forms demonstrates that the ancient Hebrews composed psalms for many different types of prayer and worship services and settings. Finally, we survey some current translations of the psalms.

POETRY IN THE PSALMS

Poetry in any language defies neat and simple description, but most people, by careful listening or reading, can recognize poetic pieces in their own language. Telltale clues of poetry in English include regular meter and the presence of rhymes at the ends of lines. Free verse poses more of a challenge at first, because it lacks these qualities, so one must look further—to language that is compressed and crafted, that offers delights to those who pause to hear or to read a line slowly, perhaps several times. Gradually we learn that poetry need not depend on rhyme and meter alone, but rather on the rhythms of sounds and the rich connotations issuing forth from words and images of the artist.

Let us examine the poetic language in Psalm 6, a psalm attributed to David but easily connected with many other people both in the Bible and in contemporary life.

2   Do not reprove me in your anger, LORD,
     nor punish me in your wrath.
3   Have pity on me, LORD, for I am weak;
     heal me, LORD, for my bones are trembling.
4   In utter terror is my soul—
     and you, LORD, how long...?
5   Turn, LORD, save my life;
     in your mercy rescue me....
7   I am wearied with sighing;
     all night long tears drench my bed;
     my couch is soaked with weeping.
8   My eyes are dimmed with sorrow,
     worn out because of all my foes. (RNAB)

In this psalm we hear the "misery" of one who prays to God. "I am wearied with sighing" sends a message, one that grows in the next lines: "All night long tears drench my bed; my couch is soaked with weeping." The poet has spoken about personal pain, but the drenched bed and the soaked couch hint at a further story—one we might wish to hear. Although we will never know the facts, we can feel the emotions in these words and can begin to feel the poet's anguish. A reporter would stand aside and report the evidence of moisture on the bed, dampness on the couch, without being able to determine its exact source unless he or she had witnessed the events. But we who have heard this simple plaintive voice know its source, though not all the reasons that led to the tears. In this case the compressed poetic language may teach us more than the clear descriptive language of reporters or lecturers.

POETIC LANGUAGE

Poetry somehow expresses our human experiences in words, so that the emotions and feelings are expressed by images. Two examples from Psalm 6 above demonstrate the movement. When the psalmist says "Heal me, LORD, for my bones are trembling," we may empathize with the experience of trembling bones from past experience, and then we know why the psalmist wants to command God: "Heal me." The second example requires more memory work on our part: "My eyes are dimmed with sorrow." Tears blur vision and make it difficult to see; after a while, the eyes naturally grow weary. Both of these images connect us with our body and its sensations, reminding us that the Hebrews probably did not distinguish among body, mind, and soul. Longings and desires expressed to God fill the psalms, many of them in prayers that express intense emotions that are first experienced physically and only later noted mentally.

Luis Alonso-Schökel (1996b, 45) claims that the primary language of prayer and poetry is physical feeling and emotion, which the poet formulates in imaginative language. Only later comes a conceptual translation, such as, "The speaker requests respite from fear" or "She is extremely distressed." These latter expressions, common in biblical commentaries and in books on prayer, convey little of the intense feeling expressed by the psalmist. The concept presents itself as a datum, a piece of information that one can process in a variety of ways. The image, on the other hand, either evokes something within me (corresponding to the source of the poet's expression) or it falls flat.

Poetic language, then, captures the deep-down bodily feelings of both the poet and the hearer or reader. The language in Psalm 6 helps us to feel some of the poet's anguish, if we allow it to. Poetry also is much more than the adornment of a spiritual notion or a theological statement (for example, "One can speak fully to God and expect and trust that God will respond appropriately"). An excellent example in the Book of Psalms is the Hebrew word *nephesh*, which most often appears in translations as "soul," though it also connotes "life" or "breath" or "person" or "neck." The word *soul* in a psalm reminds us of our religious upbringing, but we can hardly connect the poetry with emotions or feelings we have experienced, since the soul is—we have learned—incorporeal. This word *nephesh* appears in Psalm 31, a psalm of complaint of a suffering innocent person. The various ways it is translated show the differences between poetic images and expository speech. In verse 8 the words *bezarot naphshi* are translated as "you have taken heed of my adversities" or you "observed my distress" (RNAB)—both fairly abstract notions. If *nephesh* literally refers to the neck, then we might hear in the words "they are at my very neck" an expression most English speakers would connect with feelings of fear and dread.

PRAYING WITH POETIC IMAGES

Attention to the feelings expressed in the poetry of the psalms links us with the psalmists through our imagination and memories of our past experiences. Prayer lodges within the very feelings that we struggle to express to God once we have recognized them. The best way to engage these images is to hear them articulated aloud so that they evoke feelings within us. To do this in our own practice may require that we read verses slowly and attentively, that we focus on the sounds and feelings of words, and, in the process of *lectio divina*, allow ourselves to ruminate on them and to savor them. We may need to hear the verse read aloud by another, or in a different language, or set to music, or repeated over and over again, in order to let the words or images touch us deeply, in our body at least as much as in our mind.

POETIC PARALLELISM

Studies of Hebrew poetry generally devote attention to parallelism. In the Hebrew Bible many verses of two (or three) clauses or half-verses repeat the basic notion of the first part in the second. In Psalm 6 we find such repetition in verses 6 and 7.

> 6 For who among the dead remembers you?
>   Who praises you in Sheol?
> 7 I am wearied with sighing;
>   all night long tears drench my bed;
>   my couch is soaked with weeping. (RNAB)

In verse 6 the psalmist addresses God, while the following verses speak of personal anguish. First, the psalmist tries to motivate God to give concrete assistance by repeating a rhetorical question, asking, in other words, "what will happen to your praise if I am allowed to die?" At first glance, either half of the verse seems sufficient to get the idea across, yet the psalmist speaks twice in similar fashion but not in the same words. The poet first asks "who remembers you" among the dead? Is the psalmist only interested in memories of God? If we hear the next line, we get a hint: "Who praises you in Sheol?" *Sheol* is a biblical word for the underworld, the abode of the dead; perhaps the word *Sheol* links up with "among the dead" in the previous line. If so, the two verbs might also be related to each other: "remembers you" to "praises you." Not only will the psalmist have a memory of God, but he or she can "remember" God aloud, with words and song and praise—drawing on the "praise" of the next line. Hearing the two lines together reinforces an appreciation of the place—Sheol is the abode of those who have died. It also deepens a sense of the action—remembering God includes praising God. The two half-verses help to define each other's terms, but they do this without the precise language of definition (such as "Sheol is the abode of the dead"). Parallelism of language and images allows us to hear separate parts together, to compare and sift and sort them, so that each part gains richness of expression from the other.

Very often the verses in parallel reinforce each other in expressing similar feelings or notions by their images. Consider the following two examples from Psalm 13.

> 2 How long, LORD? Will you utterly forget me?
>   How long will you hide your face from me?
>   (RNAB)

How can I know that God has utterly forgotten me? How do I know the mind of God? Or is it a feeling that weighs heavily upon me? The second part draws on an experience, that God's face has been hidden from me. To "see

God's face" often indicated an experience of God in worship, so this image hints that the psalmist cannot feel God's presence when he or she prays in a shrine or the temple, alone or with others of the community. Without pretending to know the inner workings of God's mind, this psalmist articulates a recurring personal experience, one which leads to a feeling of being totally forgotten by God. Both parts of the verse can deepen our sense of the psalmist's feeling, because the two expressions reflect a similar experience and reinforce each other even through their differences. Scripture scholars have called this *synonymous parallelism*, because both sets of words and the individual words in each set act as synonyms. Here both parts of a verse play off each other and give greater resonance and richness to the feeling tone experienced when hearing either word or verse.

Another type of parallelism pits opposite images, concepts, and ideas in different parts of the same verse. In Psalm 20, verses 8 and 9 offer examples of this type of parallelism.

8   Some rely on chariots, others on horses,
         but we on the name of the LORD our God.
9   They collapse and fall,
         but we stand strong and firm. (RNAB)

In each of these verses, the first half and the second half express opposite notions. In verse 8 people rely on radically different aspects of reality, while verse 9 demonstrates the antithetical nature of their final outcomes. The antithesis between the two groups of people increases because of their interplay in two successive verses. Irony may also exist in the arrangement. Those who relied on horses and chariots were not the ones who finally stood strong and firm; rather, those who may have been ridiculed for putting all their hope in God's name did not collapse and fall, as predicted. This parallelism of opposites also emphasizes, reshapes, and enhances certain images and ideas for the discerning listener or reader.

To appreciate the impact of poetic parallelism in the psalms, one should deliberately proceed in a countercultural fashion. For example, those who take college entrance exams know that if they hope to score well, they must learn to recognize synonyms and antonyms quickly and efficiently. They should never pause to enjoy and relish the poetry of the words! The poetry of the psalms touches us quite differently. When we are able to slow down, engage our imaginations, and play the different words and images against one another within ourselves, then we will "score high" in perceiving the poet's expression.

Consider another example from Psalm 13.

> 3 a, b How long must I carry sorrow in my soul,
> grief in my heart day after day? (RNAB)

"How long" indicates that the poet wants it to stop, wants some immediate action. It is not repeated in the second part of verse 3; rather, the psalmist paints a similar emotion by asking about the time length: "day after day." If either expression of impatience is not completely clear in itself, the combination of the two binds it all together. As the poet moves through time, hearers may wonder about "sorrow in my soul" and how it relates to "grief in my heart." Perhaps grief escalates the feeling of sorrow a bit. But are "soul" and "heart" so clearly synonymous? We can probably feel grief in our heart—perhaps a tightening, a stepped-up pulse, a heaviness that is palpable. But can we say the same of our soul? This is more difficult. We should remember that the Hebrew word for soul can also mean "neck," a part of the body that often hurts and tightens when we experience deep sorrow. Either part of this verse hints at these feelings and how they emerge from our bodies. Taken together they offer far richer fare for imagination and prayer.

PRAYING WITH PARALLELS IN POETRY

In the case of images, we suggest pausing to look at and ponder a word and its image, to gaze at it with questions and admiration. But we cannot begin to perceive still more meanings until we have compared the two parts of the verse—hearing their differences, reveling in their similarities, perceiving the tone of each. The point is not to create a problem to be solved, but rather to suggest two different approaches to the language of poetry in prayer. The images, feelings, and beauty of word pictures emerge either with a long, loving gaze and contemplation or with playful comparison in the imagination and mind. No two people are alike, and no two prayer sessions are exactly alike, even for the same person. Try each focus as you desire. If you practice a kind of *lectio divina*, you might focus on single words for a reading or two, and another time let the verses or parts of verses play on each other. Wherever you begin, experience how lovely repetition can be—returning to an image from a different angle, with a different feeling or perspective. The poet's artistry allows us to enjoy the word in many different ways and in different parts of our body. If we are looking only for theological concepts, we will not likely return to this same treasury of words often, preferring to discover other concepts and to link them together. But the psalms invite continual return and promise ever renewed delights to those with time and taste, and their poetic expression keeps calling us back to experience their music and images.

GENRES OR TYPES OF PSALM PRAYER

We have found great fruit in beginning our exploration by attending to various types of worship and prayer in the psalms. Early in the twentieth century a new approach to psalms study rose to prominence: study of genres or types of psalms. Herman Gunkel found the historical approach—searching for the events behind the biblical texts—not very helpful for understanding psalms, so he paid special attention to the kinds of language and the special function of types of psalms. He showed that there are different kinds of psalms in the collection: psalms of praise for God, of thanksgiving to God, psalms that cry out to God in petition (laments), and psalms that beg for forgiveness for sin. Some psalms seem to have come directly from Israel's worship—entrance songs and processional psalms. Because some psalms seemed to contain the voice of a single individual, while others clearly represented a group singing or praying together, he spoke of individual and communal psalms (for example, individual laments, communal thanksgivings). Thus it became easier to imagine psalms in the everyday life of ordinary Israelites, who went to shrines and to the temple to beg God to take action when they were suffering, to thank God for experiences of aid, and to praise God in worship of the Creator and Redeemer.

Gunkel supposed that most psalms of a certain type used similar vocabulary, language, and images, so he compared similar-sounding psalms in his description of various categories: hymns of praise, psalms of thanksgiving, songs of trust, royal songs, laments, didactic psalms, and wisdom psalms. Some scholars continue to fine-tune these categories, but the real significance of the types is their contribution to an understanding of Israel's worship. Each type of psalm picks up the language, mood, and concerns of different moments in worship. Many find a correspondence between types of worship and their spiritual lives, so these different ways of singing Israel's psalms can also inform our prayer lives. Situations of crisis and loss interweave with times for praising God in the lives of individuals and communities; moments of gratitude and times of repentance each touch us in different ways.

In Israel, as well as in the Christian churches, different styles of worship and prayer seem better fitted to various needs. The first Catholic biblical scholar to use Gunkel's insights was a Trappist monk, Pius Drijvers. He translated many of Gunkel's important insights into ordinary language, and he provided examples from the prayer and hymnody of the Mass to demonstrate how contemporary Christians use many of the same worship forms. For our part, we find great fruit in the variety of psalms in the Bible, and in this book we describe some major types of psalms and with each of them suggest different ways of prayer suited to various moods and needs, fears and hopes.

In chapters 3 through 8, we introduce various psalm types so that they are more accessible for prayer, both corporate and personal. Each section sets the psalms of one type in their probable cultural, religious, and liturgical contexts in ancient Israel. We then comment in a more detailed way on one psalm of that type. Often we illustrate the significance of the type by relating it to parallel situations in contemporary life.

TRANSLATIONS OF THE PSALMS

We recommend that you use your favorite translation of the psalms. But we have found that a second translation can alert us to subtle differences in images and diction, and occasionally to major variations in translation.

The Psalms: New American Bible, Revised Edition (RNAB) appeared in 1991. Psalm citations in chapter 1 come from this version. The translators were biblical scholars, including members of monastic orders and specialists in English poetry. They attempted to render the psalms into an English that would be more poetic, especially for group recitation and musical settings. Moreover, with the concerns of many worshiping communities in mind, they preferred gender-inclusive language wherever possible. Language about human beings is inclusive (often mentioned in a footnote) and the God-language uses fewer masculine pronouns than comparable translations, including the NRSV. Single-volume editions of this version are available from the Catholic Book Publishing Company and Liturgical Press.

An ecumenical project of the National Council of Churches produced *The New Revised Standard Version* (NRSV); currently, it is one of the most widely used translations in the United States. We regularly cite psalm texts from this translation in this book, and all unmarked citations are from the NRSV. This translation, like its ancestors, the *Revised Standard Version* and the *King James Version*, attempts to render a consistent translation by representing every word and phrase in the Hebrew text. In terms of poetic language it does not resemble the *King James Version*, which many still consider the measuring rod for poetic psalm language. The NRSV translation, focused on needs of congregations (for proclamation) and students (for study), is not particularly poetic in language or diction. The language about human beings is gender inclusive, but the God-language seems less adapted.

The *ICEL Psalter* (1994), a translation commissioned by the International Commission on English in the Liturgy, takes a more decided turn toward liturgical language; its team included poets and scholars in English literature as well as liturgists and biblical specialists. This attempt at crisp, poetic language has met with some criticism, because it often renders notions or images or ideas from the Hebrew rather than discrete words. This translation also offers gender-inclusive language for human beings plus some creative poetic renderings of God-language.

Finally, we mention the Grail translation of the Psalms. First completed in 1963, it paid special attention to the rhythmic structures of Hebrew poetry and attempted to reproduce its effects in English. Joseph Gelineau, S.J., composed musical settings for this entire psalter, and they became widely known and loved at the precise time when Roman Catholics were rediscovering the psalms in English at their worship. The beauty of these combined settings and translation still attracts many. The Grail translation has long appeared in English versions of the Liturgy of the Hours. In 1983 an inclusive-language version of this translation appeared; it features inclusive nouns for humans but retains masculine pronouns for the deity.

A pocket-sized edition of the Psalms and a Bible in a different translation will prove to be good companions for your journey into the world of the psalms. In the next chapter we introduce a variety of prayer styles for the Book of Psalms.

Two
Approaching the Psalms: Five Styles of Prayer

The power of the psalms to transform can grow in proportion to the avenues for the psalms to take root. We can say or sing the psalm aloud; we can add the gestures mentioned in the psalm or other movements that the psalm evokes; we can write the text of the psalm, as calligraphers have done for thousands of years. This chapter introduces five ways to respond prayerfully through psalms: *lectio divina* for individuals and groups, daily prayer (the Office), handmade midrash, bodily movement to psalms, and psalm-based hymnody. These introductions provide the background for the prayer exercises found at the ends of the remaining chapters. Use as much or little of this background material as you find helpful.

LECTIO DIVINA:
AN ANCIENT WAY OF PRAYING

A very old form of Christian prayer called *lectio divina* (divine reading) matured in the ambiance of monasticism, a setting in which psalm prayer became standardized into a regular pattern for communal prayer. It can be adapted to individual and corporate psalm prayer.

Lectio divina has four movements that can be woven together in any sequence suggested by the individual prayer's interaction with the Holy Spirit. These movements are called *lectio, meditatio, oratio,* and *contemplatio* (reading, meditating, praying, and contemplating).

As in all prayer, a period of preparation gets us ready for what follows. In our overly full and highly complex lives, we often need some time to focus, to become aware that we are about to engage in a time of prayer, to still the insistent clamor within our heads, to awaken and tone the body, to call on the presence and power of the Holy Spirit, who, Christians understand, authors all prayer. Do not rush through the preparation time to get to the "real" prayer—the preparation grounds everything that follows.

The first action in divine reading is reading, not so much for content as for depth. Read and reread until the passage takes on a kind of resonance, an ambiance, a mood. A particular word or phrase may begin to draw your attention, to stand out, to become concentrated with energy, to "shimmer." Let your attention go to this word or phrase and allow it to become the doorway into greater depth and intimacy with God.

For most of us, reading means running our eyes over the printed page and drawing from the printed symbols the meaning conveyed by the words and their syntax, usually as quickly and accurately as possible. But now imagine that you are a poet. You craft the space between sound and silence; you work sleight-of-hand between literal and figurative meaning. For you, to read as quickly as possible is anathema. Further, poetry must be read aloud, or it becomes dry as dust. Poetry arises in the interaction between sound and meaning, and as poetry, the psalms come alive in the same interaction.

The ancients had not yet developed the relationship between the eye and the word on the page such that they bypassed speech. The ancients read the way poets might read today, aloud. For contemporary persons, reading aloud has an unsuspected benefit: It connects us to two more senses, the kinesthetic forming of the words with the mouth, lips, tongue, and vocal cords, and the hearing of the sounds produced. Our seeing, speaking, and hearing draw us back into our bodies as we pray. *Lectio* may be sung as well. Perhaps the words of a psalm echo a chorus or a hymn learned as a child. These passages associated with music evoke emotional resonances not available even to the spoken word.

A second "moment" in the process of *lectio divina* invites the engagement of the mind and can prove particularly rich for those for whom thinking is the primary way they process reality. Here we ruminate or "turn over" the word, phrase, or concept evoked in the *lectio* moment to see what richness might lie there waiting to be discovered.

A vivid image popular among the ancients illustrates this aspect. The rumen is the first of several stomach compartments of cows and other ruminants. When a cow chews its cud, it regurgitates the contents from one compartment, remasticates it, and swallows it into another compartment, greatly enhancing the process of breaking down the tough fiber of its forage. In *lectio*, one ruminates, turns over the material, and views it from all sides. Any connections in the text to other parts of scripture, or to personal experience, work to "digest" the text and break it open for our own personal encounter with the living God.

Sooner or later the meditation evokes a personal response to God, whether question, angry rejoinder, praise, gratitude, plea for help, or any of the infinite possibilities of exchange between one person and another. The address of *oratio* is personal and immediate.

Finally, *lectio* stills us into a wordless mode of communication: *contemplatio* (contemplation). This aspect consists of resting in God's presence, allowing God to uphold, nourish, love, heal, teach, and challenge us as God sees fit. It may consist of a brief moment or it may expand to become the primary dynamic of the prayer.

At any moment of this process our attention may wander, or our energy or nourishment dry up. When this occurs, simply return to *lectio* and repeat the reading. Another word or phrase may garner attention, or perhaps not. In any case, the continual repetition of *lectio* serves to rein in our roving attention and to implant the words of the text deeply in our hearts and minds, where they can continue to transform us. Another day, another small bite of scripture, thoroughly digested, may nourish us.

The process need not move in the order presented; one may move from *lectio* directly to *oratio* or to *contemplatio*, then back to *meditatio*, then back to *lectio*—or any other possible combination—as the Spirit leads. Notice the significant role the body plays, your physical feelings, as well as words and images. Varying your posture in different parts of *lectio divina* can yield different fruits. Experiment. Do what seems to facilitate your immediate and personal interaction with God. There is no "correct" way to pray, though this method, as others, offers us some wisdom and guidance.

Finally, at the end of *lectio divina* take a few moments to write down the major movements that you experienced. For example, you might note the text you selected; the word, phrase, image, or concept that caught your attention; one or two of the thoughts or ruminations that occurred to you; the tone or feeling evoked by any moments of contemplation; and the central focus of your response. Such a journal entry might be about the length of a paragraph. Sometimes the act of writing opens new levels of prayer.

LECTIO DIVINA AS GROUP PRAYER

Thus far we have treated *lectio divina* as a prayer for individuals, but it lends itself to powerful corporate prayer as well. The exercise below is ideal for groups of four to eight persons. It can be adapted for larger groups as well, though in larger groups it may prove difficult for all to speak aloud.

First, the leader selects the passage to be prayed together. The group may find relatively short selections filled with concrete images more accessible than long or abstract passages. The psalms offer many powerful passages ideal for communal *lectio divina*. Before beginning, the leader may arrange with one or two other persons to read the psalm later in the process. It is sometimes helpful if the voices alternate between men's and women's and among several translations.

The leader assists the group members to come to silence and recollection and gives whatever brief directions are necessary to the process. Next follows *lectio*, reading the psalm slowly all the way through. After a pause, the same passage is read a second time, again at a gentle, reflective pace. Another pause, this time of some minutes. Each group member continues the *lectio* interiorly, seeking the word or phrase that beckons. After a suitable amount of time, the leader invites each participant to share his or her word or phrase aloud. The other members of the group receive that word into themselves without comment. The pace here, as throughout the group *lectio divina*, is deliberate. It is like dropping a pebble into a pond: One waits until the ripples have reached the edges of the pond before another pebble is dropped into the depth.

The text is read again (a third time), with perhaps a different reader and translation. This reading signals the movement to *meditatio*. With simple directions the leader invites the group members to use the silence to turn over their words and phrases, to ruminate, to ponder. After a suitable amount of time the leader invites those who wish to share, briefly and simply, something that arose for them during the time of meditation. Again, these sharings are received in silence by the other members of the group.

The text is read a fourth time. This time the leader invites the group to contemplative and somewhat more extended silence, opening to the presence of God through not only their own meditation but also the rich collage that has been created by the group sharing. Participants may be invited to journal or simply to rest in God's embrace. Finally, the leader invites the members to *oratio*, to simple prayers voiced aloud. The leader then "collects" the group members into a final prayer.

The process may be extended or abbreviated according to the needs and desires of the group. Variations are certainly possible. Many groups like to conclude with a time of intercessory prayer, for example.

Lectio divina, whether in individual or group form, invites participants to a deep experience of the word of God opening out into the Word of God addressed to each one, here and now. Its long, vibrant history attests to its flexibility and its appeal to a broad variety of persons. Suggestions for *lectio divina* with psalms are included at the conclusions of chapters 3–10.

MORNING AND EVENING PRAYER: A COMMON TRADITION

Corporate praying of the psalms, or the Divine Office, as it came to be called, has a long history in the Christian tradition. Its roots extend back before Christ into Judaism, where a pattern of morning and evening prayer developed around the temple sacrifices. Morning and evening prayer, including psalms, was also important in the synagogue and in personal prayer. Jesus himself probably prayed the psalms in this way, and the first Christians quite readily continued this practice as they gathered in his memory. The prayers referred to in Acts 2:42 are probably services of morning and evening prayer held in individual homes. To these early Christians, themselves Jews, the psalms pointed prophetically to Christ, so they experienced no disjunction using these "Jewish" texts in their own prayer (*Daily Prayer* 1987, 15). Gradually the structure of daily prayer became more formalized. It evolved in two parallel settings, cathedral and monastery. However, both traditions eventually became so elaborate that lay participation dwindled in favor of easier substitutes. One substitute that grew up in the Middle Ages was the Rosary, with the 150 beads representing the 150 psalms.

The Protestant reformers, particularly in Germany, desired to revive the general practice of morning and evening prayer and make it normative. They were also anxious to reinstate the psalms as a source of personal and corporate prayer. Consequently, the psalter was soon translated into vernacular languages and arranged for singing by the whole congregation. By the end of the sixteenth century in Protestant areas, daily psalm prayer was based in the family as the "new monastery." The day began with Morning Prayer and the night meal concluded with Evening Prayer, each following the basic structure that daily psalm prayer has had from its origins to this day, namely, singing a psalm, listening to scripture, and making intercessions.

In recent years, in response to the upsurge of biblical scholarship and liturgical renewal, psalm-based daily prayer is again undergoing a revival. The outlines of Morning Prayer and Evening Prayer from the *Book of Common Worship* (1993, 490, 504) provide a simple order of service, similar in most traditions.

Morning Prayer	*Evening Prayer*
Opening Sentences	Service of Light
	Opening Sentences
Morning Hymn	Hymn to Christ the Light
	Thanksgiving for Light
	Evening Psalm (141)
	Psalm Prayer
	or
	Opening Sentences
	Evening Hymn
Psalm(s)	Psalm(s)
Psalm	Psalm
Silent Prayer	Silent Prayer
[Psalm Prayer]	[Psalm Prayer]
Scripture Reading	Scripture Reading
Silent Reflection	Silent Reflection
[A brief interpretation or non-biblical reading]	[A brief interpretation or non-biblical reading]
Canticle of Zechariah (or other canticle)	Canticle of Mary (or other canticle)
Prayer of Thanksgiving and Intercession	Prayer of Thanksgiving and Intercession

Concluding Prayer	Concluding Prayer
Lord's Prayer	Lord's Prayer
[Hymn or Spiritual]	[Hymn or Spiritual]
Dismissal	Dismissal
[Sign of Peace]	[Sign of Peace]

Night Prayer (Compline) employs a similar outline, with the addition of a few minutes for examination of conscience, a review of one's day before God. Its canticle comes from Luke 2:29–32, the lovely prayer of Simeon, "Now you dismiss your servant."

Short scripture readings may be selected by following a lectionary or by continuous reading through a book of the Bible, a tradition encouraged and preserved in the Reformation churches. Materials in brackets may be included if desired. Hymns may be selected to fit the community or the liturgical season, as well as the time of day.

When a person is worshiping alone or in a family group, or when circumstances call for an abbreviated order, the following generally serves well:

Psalm
Scripture Reading
Silent Reflection
Prayers of Thanksgiving and Intercession

This simplified order allows the pray-er to proceed thoughtfully through a smaller amount of biblical material. *Lectio divina* can enrich this personal prayer. A family with small children can employ one or two verses of a psalm, a minute of silence, and one or two verses of another scripture reading, with as many intercessory and thanksgiving prayers as are timely and interesting for small children. Once the pattern is familiar to the worshiping community, its regularity and rhythm ground the praying community, yet the liturgical options keep it fresh and inviting.

Various styles of reciting or singing the psalms allow for variety and accommodate the musical ability of the congregation. The leader may choose from any of the following: (1) *direct*, chanting or reciting the psalm straight through; (2) *antiphonal*, verse-by-verse alternation between groups, such as between the choir and congregation or between one side of the congregation and the other; (3) *responsorial*, the verses are sung by a cantor or choir, with the congregation singing a refrain after each verse or group of verses; (4) *responsive*, verse-by-verse alternation between the presider and the congregation (*Lutheran Book of Worship* 1978, 20). Local circumstances will suggest the optimum balance between change and consistency.

One further pastoral situation needs comment. Women sometimes find the language of the psalms difficult for their individual or corporate prayer, suggesting that inclusive-language resources for corporate prayer be used in many situations. A caution, however: Sometimes inclusive renderings omit or soften the strong or violent images in the psalms. A pastoral decision to moderate these images in the psalms may leave the impression that inclusive communities need not mirror in their prayer these harsher realities. We will cover this pastoral issue when we discuss imprecatory psalms.

A worshiping community gains much from regular psalm-based Morning Prayer and Evening Prayer. First, it will grow in a specifically biblical spirituality. Regular praying of the psalms, especially by singing, builds an expanded repertoire of prayers learned by heart. The prayer language of the psalms infiltrates our own individual and corporate prayer, gradually giving it depth and breadth. Second, the psalms lend themselves to group use.

They may be sung in a variety of settings, metrically, in chant, or responsorily. The prayers at the conclusion of each psalm express in the worshiper's own words the essence of the psalm, allowing for the particular needs of various groups. Third, the community can share leadership and gain broad participation. Leadership does not depend on the presence of clergy, and even quite small children can take part, encouraging direct ownership of corporate prayer by the pray-ers. Fourth, psalm-based prayer can be adapted to a variety of circumstances, both of time and composition of the worshiping community. From family prayer to regular staff gatherings to special retreats, prayer with psalms can easily be employed. Finally, and perhaps most significantly, such prayer provides a structure that can be made more or less elaborate as pastoral needs dictate. When everyone is tired, overworked, too pressed for time, or too depleted of creative ideas to prepare an original communal prayer, the structure of Morning Prayer and Evening Prayer can keep a group praying, corporately and biblically.

Psalm-based Morning Prayer and Evening Prayer are not the exclusive property of one or other Christian denomination but have developed in a variety of ways across the range of Roman, Anglican, Protestant, and Orthodox churches. The psalms truly have been the prayer book of the entire Christian community.

HANDMADE MIDRASH: PRAYING VISUALLY

Jewish midrash, or free exposition of a biblical text, can be an avenue that links the biblical text to our own experience and illumines both our experience and the text, often in fresh and surprising ways. The exercises suggested by the title "Handmade Midrash" call upon a visual language that precedes words. These exercises, created by Jo Milgrom, specialist in art and Jewish spirituality, invite us to set aside normal modes of thought to see things in a new way. The creativity unleashed does not depend upon prior experience with art. Handmade midrash should be seen not primarily as art but as prayer—though the results may prove surprisingly artistic.

The tasks are utterly simple, such as tearing paper or muslin, working with clay, or penciling various kinds of lines to explain a text more fully. The process bypasses the critical consciousness and allows fragments of fantasy and creativity to emerge. The forms are produced through "play," but they always mean something, evoked as they are through the interactions among text, personal experience, and conversation with others and with oneself. As hidden forms and feelings emerge, so too do new levels of the biblical text (Milgrom 1992, 6–7).

The process has several steps:

1. Study the biblical text. Some questions centering around the essence of the biblical passage help focus the hands-on creative process. For example, in pondering Psalm 142:8, we might wonder what it is like to be in the prison.

2. If possible, study related art, observing some ways others have interpreted this text visually.

3. Do hands-on, creative art play. Simple materials and processes become the media of the work. Many people feel they can participate more freely if they are instructed not to try to create anything representational, such as a figure, a face, or any other recognizable form. Media may vary: two or more colors of construction paper, which are torn (without implements) and pasted in relationship to one

another; pencil or ink on white or colored paper; old fabric and notions, with glue for assembling; any writing or coloring medium upon a background of choice; modeling clay; other simple materials that may be found around the home, such as rice or seeds, dried weeds or flowers, buttons, nails, wire, toothpicks, paper bags, tissue paper, and so on.

4. After the creative work is done, meet with one other person (or a small group). Describe to one another what you have done and what it means. Do as many of the following as seem helpful:

- Ask someone else to describe what he or she sees in what you have done.
- What was the hardest or the easiest form to make? Why?
- Discuss the role that color plays in your creation.
- Notice sizes, proportion, movement. How do the parts relate? What do the parts mean?
- Would you now change any part of your creation?
- With which element do you identify?
- Connect the visual creation to the text and notice what, if anything, changes.

5. Write, using as many of the following approaches as are helpful:

- Free associate, allowing images and thoughts to surface and to be expressed.
- Bring opposites together. For example, in Psalm 142 think of bound and free as closely related rather than as opposites.
- Look for correspondences between your creation and your inner thoughts and feelings.
- Look for balance of feeling, form, and concept. Does one figure dominate? Does the totality obscure the detail? Can the whole emerge through a part?

6. How has the visual experience of the handmade midrash affected your earlier interpretations of the text? Reflect on the most important thing that occurred for you in creating the handmade midrash in relation to the text (Milgrom 1992, 11).

More levels may emerge from your handmade midrash. Milgrom suggests that returning to your writing after a few days may bring forth further insight.

One of the participants in a handmade midrash workshop made the following comment: "I discovered that as an observer, I would be confined to interpretation, but as a participant, I was open to God's power" (Milgrom 1992, 139). Engaging the mind and heart through the visual process of handmade midrash can bring the psalms alive in unexpected ways.

WORSHIPFUL MOVEMENT: PRAYING WITH THE BODY

The psalms (RNAB used here) literally cry out for bodily expression: "Give praise with tambourines and dance" (Ps 150:4); "I bow low towards your holy temple" (Ps 138:2); "By the rivers of Babylon we sat mourning and weeping" (Ps 137:1); "To you I raise my eyes, to you enthroned in heaven" (Ps 123:1); "I lie prostrate in the dust" (Ps 119:25); "All you peoples, clap your hands" (Ps 47:1); "Enter, let us bow down in worship: let us kneel before the LORD who made us" (Ps 95:6). These phrases suggest the range of bodily involvement encouraged by the psalms. As noted musician and liturgist Lucien Deiss says: "No other prayer invites the community so often to associate body and soul in prayer: prostrating oneself, lifting one's hands, moving forward with cries of joy, processing around the altar. At least we affirm in the psalms that we do these" (1996, 113). Reality is often much different. In our personal prayer we usually read a psalm silently while sitting still, assuming that this is how to pray.

Because of our presuppositions about prayer, many persons ask, "Why move in prayer?" We move to express the intimate connection between body and self. We *are* our bodies, we do not simply *have* bodies. We move to create the kinesthetic learning and memory that, for some, is their primary way of receiving information and processing it. We move to bring alive our inner dialogue; *emotion*, after all, is literally "e-motion" or "motion out of." The body is the home of emotion, and emotion is the "motor" of living, breathing, life-changing, prayerful living. Without the body, our prayer is disembodied, desiccated, incomplete.

Movement in prayer and worship is a contentious issue in many situations. It shares many of the issues raised by liturgical dance. Cynthia Winton-Henry, a liturgical dancer and minister, has reflected on this problem at some length in the course of her work with individuals, ensembles, and congregations. Movement and dance, she notes, give us ways to image, name, and express power and its illusion. Consequently, they can be very threatening to those who seek control. When authorities attempt to ban dancing, it simply goes underground and moves to more tolerant environments: studios, recreation centers, theaters, nightclubs, and the streets. Dance provides one of the primary ways that indigenous and other ethnic peoples maintain their identity in the face of pressure to assimilate into dominant cultures. Thus, when Israel became a nation, the government immediately sponsored the creation of new songs and dances to build national and religious identity.

People who dance with one another discover they are one (Winton-Henry 1989, 4–6, 11).

Movement and dance attract and threaten because they communicate relationship to earth, humans, and other creatures. Dancers need to be held and lifted, to reach out, to run with, to follow, to lead, to stand alone, and to join together. Both the liberating and confining aspects of all these relational experiences appear in the dance, not only among dancers but also between dancers and audience. Dance also reveals sexuality, even when dancers are fully clothed and circumspect in their action—it cannot be otherwise if dance is the art form of the body. Though traditional theology affirms the goodness of creation and therefore of bodies, this is contradicted in much of what we do and resist doing with our bodies in prayer and worship. Movement and dance have the potential both to reveal the West's longstanding split between body and spirit and to offer a contribution to its healing (Winton-Henry 1989, 6–11).

Granting ourselves permission to move at the level at which we are comfortable seems to be an important key to freeing ourselves to begin to move in prayer and worship. Consequently, all movement suggestions offered as prayer options in this book come with this caveat: Do only what you feel comfortable doing, and omit (or in a group situation, wait out) those actions for which you do not feel ready. At the same time, however, it is good to stretch your comfort zone a little.

Improvisation, or spontaneous creation of movement or dance, can help us begin to move within our prayer. Winton-Henry offers four simple steps in improvisation: observe, bring yourself, be responsible, and come as a guest of silence. Observing is simple but significant. Practice observing. Walk around a room or park or block. Notice all that there is to observe. Then close your eyes and "take a walk around yourself" (1985, 9). The second step, to bring yourself, means allowing all that you are to come with you into your experience of movement: body, personality, experiences, culture, and religious traditions. These structures can free us if we intentionally explore them and allow the truths that lie in them to surface. To be responsible, the third step, means the ability to give back. To whom? To God, who is in the mundane as well as the significant, in the persons around us, in their pains and joys. Finally, we come to movement as a "guest of silence." In the realm of movement, stillness is the reflection of silence. Stillness is the inevitable first and last moment of any movement. Stillness is as essential to movement as silence is to spoken prayer (Winton-Henry 1985, 8–12).

These insights can help us begin to move, but how do we begin to move *as prayer*, especially those of us who have never considered our bodies as integral to prayer? *Lectio divina*, so central to our appropriation of the psalms in our personal and corporate prayer, can give us a path. The relationship of *lectio divina* to movement prayer was revealed to us in one of our psalms retreats. We asked Dominican Sister Martha Starret, liturgist and dancer, "How do you figure out how to dance to a psalm?" Her answer, transcribed from a brief talk developed as a reply to our question, follows.

> The way I prepare for dance is the same method of *lectio divina*. I just begin to listen to the song, just let it begin to sing itself inside me. Maybe you have done that—you have a song and you just keep listening to it and it touches you. Or poetry, or just plain instrumental music, or some prose that you read, or some scripture. Something begins to touch you.
>
> So I just begin to listen to it, the whole song, and then after I have listened to it for a while I begin to

allow myself to be drawn to the phrases and the words that shimmer inside. You know them; you know what words begin to speak to you and to speak to your experience. Just sit with them, very quietly. I don't always sit patiently, because I would like the movement to come faster. But I just keep repeating them, as in *lectio divina*, just the phrase, just the word.

And then, after I have listened to it maybe three or four or five or sometimes ten times, I begin to feel something in my body. In the case of dance, I am letting a word interact with my body. Again, it is sitting with the word or phrase and waiting for images to come about how I will use my hands or where I turn. Oftentimes I begin to relate it to my own experience, and each time I dance it, it may be another life experience that I am dancing.

Be gentle with yourself and listen to yourself as you pray, and notice—just notice—if you are feeling God's word somewhere in your body. If you want to raise your arms in praise, can you give yourself permission to raise your arms in praise? And you may not; this may not be a way that is comfortable for you.

I call this *lectio divina with body praise*. You may want to try it as you sit with the word and listen to it, and it begins to unfold inside you. There may be a feeling that comes: maybe anger—how would you express that with movements? Fear—how would you express that? Praise? Joy? Love? And the movements don't have to be exactly what I have just showed you. They can be your own expression.

We express a lot with our bodies. A great deal of body language goes on every day. We are always moving, unless we are asleep. And even then we are still moving: heart is still beating, blood is still pumping, we turn, we toss, eyelids flutter. So there's always body movement, and sometimes we can just make that body movement more intentional in praise.

I encourage you to sit with the word, to listen, and then to listen to your body, and then just to be aware of images that come of you dancing and moving with it. Take a psalm that particularly strikes you. Maybe just find a phrase, and sit with it, and listen and wait to see if your body wants to express that phrase in movement. It's that simple. (Starrett 1998)

PSALM HYMNODY: SINGING THE PSALMS

Psalm literally means "to make music." As religious prayer and poetry, a psalm is, by definition, meant to be sung or accompanied by an instrument (Prévost 1997, 56). To read the psalms silently or even to say them aloud reduces the psalm in a manner analogous to reading silently or reciting aloud the lyrics of a rock song or the oratorio *Messiah*: We get a bit of the impact, but far from all of it. Fortunately, an increasing number of resources can help us return to the full meaning of psalm as religious poetry played or sung.

Ancient psalms could have been played on a variety of instruments. In David's time singing involved accompaniment of lyres, harps, timbrels, and possibly even wind instruments (Sarna 1993, 8, 144). Today pianos, organs, guitars, and a variety of string and wind instruments, as well as drums, cymbals, and all kinds of other percussion instruments, both standard and improvised, accompany psalm singing. We can even have entire orchestras, courtesy of modern recording and playback, if not from the resources of each congregation.

Eventually, musicologists may accurately reconstruct what the psalms sounded like in ancient Israel. But psalms have always been played and sung, even without a living memory of the sound of the originals. The sheer volume of psalm settings throughout history is amazing. It is appropriate, then, that all musical resources be used on the psalm in Sunday liturgical settings—indeed, many of these same musical instruments are mentioned themselves in the psalms (Prévost 1997, 84).

Christian psalm singing appears to date from the earliest days, when Christians still regularly attended the synagogue. The synoptic gospels (Matt 22:43, 26:30; Mark 14:26), Acts (2:25, 4:25), Paul (Rom 4:6) and other letters (Jas 5:13; Col 3:16; Eph 5:19) all attest to psalm singing by the early Christian communities. Early Christian prayer grew out of the synagogue service, but as cultures and musical tastes changed, so did the styles of singing the psalms. Codification of much of the sung worship of the early centuries is attributed to Gregory the Great in the seventh century (hence called Gregorian chant), and it continued to be elaborated in the West long past the Protestant Reformation. The Anglican chant tradition began to diverge after the Reformation, giving rise to its own rich tradition of similar but not identical ways to sing the psalms.

In the Reformed tradition, however, the psalms truly became the congregation's prayer. With the rise of metered hymnody, the Reformed tradition also spawned a major departure from the way psalms had been rendered. In this style the psalm text was translated with attention to poetic meter so that it could be sung in hymn-like tunes. The simplicity of the metered psalm hymns fostered the widespread memorizing and singing of the psalms, precisely the goal of the Reformers. One major result of this "innovation" is the Geneva Psalter (1542), issued by John Calvin. In this psalter each psalm had its own melody, resulting in a close affinity between text and tune. In Anglican worship metrical psalms were also generally sung before and after the sermon, and so they made their way into the worship of a tradition already incorporating plainchant renderings of the psalms (Holladay 1993, 198–201, 210).

In Scotland a second method of metered psalmody developed, the most notable example being the Scottish Psalter of 1650. Here the psalms were translated into common poetic meters so that a variety of tune/hymn combinations could be used interchangeably. In this case the strictures of meter and rhyme burdened the translation, and various tunes skewed the interpretation in quite different, even contradictory ways. Awkward syntax and "flattening" of the imagery of the psalms and distortion of the mood often resulted (*The Psalter* 1993, 12). There were two American reactions to these changes. In the *Bay Psalm Book* (1640) and its long-lived successor, the *New England Psalm Book* (1651), the ministers were concerned to produce a rendering as close to the Hebrew as the meter would allow. The other reaction moved toward paraphrases and hymnody Christianizing the psalms that had been their antecedents (Holladay 1993, 206). In these paraphrases it is sometimes difficult to identify which part of scripture is being sung.

Protestant hymnody, based more or less on the psalms, flowered from the eighteenth century on. Two important figures from this era are Isaac Watts and Charles Wesley. Watts (1674–1748) deliberately Christianized his psalm paraphrases. For example, from Psalm 72 he created "Jesus Shall Reign Where'er the Sun." Psalm 98:4–9 became the beloved Christmas hymn "Joy to the World." Charles Wesley drew less from the psalms than from New Testament passages and his own experience. With these two hymn writers, hymnody began to break lose from its ties to the ancient tradition of psalm singing. A few metered psalms from the past continued to be loved and sung, but often their origin as psalms became obscured. They simply appeared as wonderful hymns among many wonderful hymns, all sharing a common repertoire of biblical images (*The Psalter* 1993, 12–14).

Recent years, however, have seen a resurgence of psalm singing. After Vatican II, with the change from Latin to the vernacular in the Roman Catholic Church, it once again became possible for the laity to sing the psalms meaningfully. But in order for lay psalm singing to take root, entirely new, easy-to-learn psalm settings needed to be composed. In the early 1950s Joseph Gelineau, a French Jesuit, developed a method upon which the new vernacular psalm settings could rely. Through what Gelineau called "sprung rhythm," he preserved the rhythmic structure inherent in Hebrew poetry; the same sprung rhythm also accommodated various vernacular languages. In this style the rhythm of the singing moves on the stressed syllables only. It therefore allows for the singing of unmetered texts (such as the psalms) without distorting the meaning by forcing their thought into the constraints of poetic meter. Gelineau based his tones on ancient psalm tones but added contemporary antiphons highlighting aspects of the psalm or a christological interpretation. Generally a choir or cantor sings the psalm, and the congregation sings the metered antiphon as a refrain. Following Gelineau, many contemporary composers continue to produce fresh and accurate renderings of the psalms. The sprung rhythm easily accommodates contemporary translations. Some newly composed metrical psalms faithfully render the mood and meaning of the biblical texts. They have the same benefits today as metrical psalms settings in the time of the Reformers; that is, they introduce psalmody into the life of the congregation and make the psalms easy to memorize and pray wholeheartedly (*The Psalter* 1993, 13).

Unmetered, pointed psalms occur in many contemporary worship resources. This system works on a simple principle. A straightforward melody (tone) of two, three, or four sections consists of dark (half) and open (whole) notes. The dark (half) notes each receive one syllable, the open (whole) notes receive all the rest of the syllables that occur up to a syllable marked with a point or mark (this mark might appear as a dot, an accent mark, or an underline, depending on the particular resource). When you reach a pointed syllable, you simply match it to the dark note. Continue matching black notes to single syllables and open notes to all the rest of the words in the verse. All the syllables and words that are sung to the open note take the rhythm and stress of ordinary speech—hence the description "unmetered." Once you get the feel for the rhythm and placement and learn a few simple tunes, you can sing the entire psalter.

Let us look at a few verses of Psalm 34 in two contemporary versions. *Worship III* (1986) suggests the following psalm tone to accompany Psalm 34:

Psalm Tone

Richard Proulx

The first few verses of the psalm appear as follows:

> I will **bless** the LORD at àll **times,**
> His **praise** always ón my **lips;**
> In the LORD my **soul** shall make ìts **boast.**
> The **humble** shall **hear** and bé **glad.**

Note that there are four sections (bars) to this psalm tone, one section (bar) for each line of the stanza. The notation consists in open and filled notes. Open notes signify that one sings as many syllables as are necessary for the sense of the text on that note, and at a pace that mimics speaking. The filled notes receive only one syllable each.

Next, note the way the text is marked (pointed) by means of accent marks. These accent marks signify where the intonation shifts; the words will indicate this shift by a similar accent mark. To sing this verse, simply begin intoning the words to the first note of the first bar of the psalm tone. When you come to the accented syllable, "àll," sing it to the dark note marked with the similar accent mark. Complete the remaining word or words from this line on the remaining note or notes of the bar. If the next note is filled, it receives only one syllable. If it is open it receives as many syllables as remain in the line. Begin intoning the second line on the first note of the second bar, moving to the accented note when you come to the accented word, "ón," and complete the line to the last notes of the bar, single syllables to filled notes, multiple syllables to the open notes. In this second line, then, one intones "ón" on the first dark, accented note, "my" on the second dark (unaccented) note, and "lips" on the final open note. Continue intoning lines three and four similarly with the notes in the third and fourth bars, respectively.

The second example of Psalm 34 comes from the *Book of Common Worship* (1993).

TONE 6 (B)

The psalm text follows, showing a slightly different convention for pointing, with accent marks above the stressed syllable:

I will **bless** the LORD at àll **times,**
His **praise** always ón my **lips;**

In the LORD my **soul** shall make its **boast.**
The **hum**ble shall **hear** and bé **glad.**

Again, begin intoning the words of the first line on the first
note of the first measure. When you come to the marked
syllable, "bléss," sing it to the first dark note. Sing "the" to
the second dark note. Complete the line "LORD," on the
next open note, in the second bar. Notice the asterisk on
the psalm verse and on the psalm tone; it signals that you
begin the next line at that place. Therefore sing "Whose"
on the open note of the next bar. Continue through the
remainder of the second line in the now-familiar pattern.
Repeat the psalm tone for the next two lines.

The suggested psalm tones usually match the genre and
mood of the psalm to which they are assigned. Actually,
with a little practice you can sing almost any psalm to
almost any psalm tone, though occasionally, for the sake
of sense, you may have to sing two syllables on one note.
When this situation occurs in a published resource, it will
usually be indicated by a "slur."

Different Christian traditions have developed varying
sensibilities about the very act of singing. Many Roman
Catholics in the United States inherited a tradition in
which hymn-singing played a small role. Reformed
Christians, on the other hand, count hymnody as one of
the richest aspects of their spiritual traditions and avidly
join in congregational singing as an important aspect of
worship, both congregational and family. Whichever tradition you belong to, we invite you to pray the psalms the
way they were meant to be prayed: by singing them.
Singing is, indeed, praying twice. Some suggestions to
develop psalm singing as personal and corporate spiritual
practice follow.

● Develop a small library of sacred music tapes and com-
pact disks that include psalm settings. Excellent contemporary resources abound; some are listed in the bibliography.

In addition, a surprisingly rich array of classical composers have used the psalms: Schütz, Monteverdi, Handel, Rachminoff, Bernstein, and many others wrote psalm settings. Play a selection (a collection or one piece) meditatively, perhaps many times. Allow the music to touch deeper and deeper aspects of yourself. Follow the playing with a time of silence and a spoken or written response to God. As the music becomes more familiar, join in the singing yourself.

• Using your congregation's hymnal, select a psalm. (We have included some suggestions from hymnals in chapters 3–10.) Sing it, perhaps several times. Let it take root in you. If you play a musical instrument, use it to accompany yourself. Or develop your own simple instruments, such as percussion and bells, and add them to your rendering at appropriate moments.

• Learn to sing the psalms in the unmetered, pointed style illustrated above and develop a practice of Morning Prayer or Evening Prayer according to your tradition's resources. While these services are primarily intended for group worship, they can provide a rich diet of psalm prayer for individuals as well. In your own personal prayer, however, never feel constrained to "finish" the prayer if your own leanings are to focus on one part.

• Set your practice of *lectio divina* to song: For every repetition, sing the psalm instead of reciting it. Try singing the psalm in various musical settings. How does the feel of the psalm change? Does it invite different responses from you?

• Allow a psalm to bubble up its own tune. You might ask yourself, as you pray, how would this psalm invite itself to be sung or played?

• In using metered psalmody, notice how the meter subtly interprets the psalm. Are there "lost" aspects of the psalm that you wish to "restore?" Your restoration might take the form of writing a new verse to the metered psalm text or even entirely new lyrics based on your own prayerful appropriation of the psalm.

• Allow a psalm to stay with you throughout the day in the form of a sung version. Simple refrains and antiphons readily lend themselves to this form of "praying always."

A group's participation in psalm singing can grow, too. The following suggestions, while they may not seem at first glance to be prayer, actually allow us to pray in the midst of other activities.

• Encourage those responsible for liturgy and worship to develop a repertoire of psalms with the choir and the congregation. These can then be sung as responsorials between the readings, and many of them can serve as hymns or anthems in their own right. Meanwhile, the psalm literacy of the entire worshiping community increases.

• Consider offering a traditional hymn-sing liberally sprinkled with psalms during or before the regular worship, or perhaps at a special service. This tradition passes on the legacy of traditional psalmody, provides a forum for teaching the new settings, and plants the phrases and music deep inside the participants, just as the Reformers in Geneva understood. A variation on this theme for those who belong to choirs: Consider choir practice as a time of prayer—all the elements of prayer are present, awaiting only your intention and desire to bear greater fruit.

• Experiment with a repertoire of ways that psalms are sung and thereby expand the possibilities for group psalm singing. Try the traditional "call and response" method, also called echo or "lining out," where the leader sings one line or verse and the responders simply repeat the same line or verse. Unless the music is very complex, everyone, even small children, can easily join in the singing. Experiment with cantors and choirs singing the more complex parts while inviting all to sing the refrains and antiphons. Note the psalm base in much traditional and contemporary hymnody, so that the singers are aware that the cadence and metaphors they are singing come to them through the psalms.

These few suggestions are meant to stimulate your imagination for your own situation. The more you look, the more you will become aware of psalms in many places. The more you see, the more you can participate in the great crowd of those who sing their praise to God.

Psalm 6

To the leader: with stringed instruments; according to The Sheminith. A Psalm of David.

1   O LORD, do not rebuke me in
      your anger,
    or discipline me in your wrath.
2   Be gracious to me, O LORD, for I
      am languishing;
    O LORD, heal me, for my bones
    are shaking with terror.
3   My soul also is struck with terror,
    while you, O LORD—how long?

4   Turn, O LORD, save my life;
    deliver me for the sake of your
      steadfast love.
5   For in death there is no
      remembrance of you;
    in Sheol who can give you
      praise?

6   I am weary with my moaning;
    everynight I flood my bed with
      tears;
    I drench my couch with my
      weeping.
7   My eyes waste away because of
      grief;
    they grow weak because of all
      my foes.
8   Depart from me, all you workers
      of evil,
    for the LORD has heard the
      sound of my weeping.
9   The LORD has heard my
      supplication;
    the LORD accepts my prayer.
10 All my enemies shall be ashamed
    and struck with terror;
    they shall turn back, and in a
      moment be put to shame.

Three

Crying Out to God in Need: Psalms of Lament

Can I be angry at God? Can I express anger in prayer? Such questions never stop surprising us, whether in pastoral ministry, spiritual direction, or conversing with friends or relatives about the important aspects of our lives. We live in an era in which many people approve—even encourage—cathartic expression of negative feelings and emotions, but complaining in prayer or articulating anger against God still makes many uncomfortable. Perhaps such an expression of anger touches something deeply ingrained in us from an early age.

That is not to say that Christians have no history of anger against God. John's grandmother knew how to let God know she was angry. Sometimes, she once wrote, in the early morning when she could not fall asleep, she would talk to God about how she felt. She would recall St. Teresa of Avila, who had told God at a particularly bleak moment, "If this is the way you treat your friends, it's no wonder you have so few of them!" John's grandmother would speak in similar words of frustration to God, and afterward she felt better. She had learned the first step of the prayer of lamentation. She would probably have many imitators today, people who transform anger into humor.

This strategy is attractive, because there is no lack of hurt and frustration in human lives.

Which of us has not at some time felt sad, confused, immobilized, unable to make a move, angry at our situation, depressed, angry with others who should have done more for us, betrayed by friends, mad at enemies, tired of illness, wondering why God lets all this happen to us? Our problems may revolve around sickness, the death of a loved one, losing a job, facing retirement. Frustration may arise from gross inequity in the ways people are treated, the injustice of our government, some experience of pain or embarrassment in the church, a natural tragedy, a personal failure, abandonment. At such times it is often hard to express precisely what we are feeling. When we complain, we often yearn for a target, someone to scream at. But since we have been socialized not to articulate anger, we usually tone it down or transform it into humor. People who complain to God seem to prefer indirect expressions of anger.

Such attitudes also help to explain a curious fact about Christian perceptions of the Book of Psalms: Although many psalms echo passionate complaining to God, most people express surprise at the suggestion that we can learn to pray about our anger and hurt from the psalms. Whether our acquaintance with the psalms comes from personal prayer and meditation or from the Liturgy of the Hours or other kinds of public prayer and worship, Christians usually remember many more psalms of praise, gratitude, and trust than psalms of complaint. Few people realize that psalms of lament far outnumber the psalms of praise and thanksgiving (Drijvers 1965).

LAMENT AS A TYPE OF PSALM

John's seminary-level course on psalms includes both Catholic and Protestant students, and usually some older ministers on sabbatical. Many have prayed the psalms regularly for many years and yearn for an opportunity to learn more about them, while others are beginners. The course is designed around the different types of psalms, as described in chapter 1, and usually begins with laments. Psalms that exhibit a mixture of sadness, anger, and helplessness usually contain concrete language directed to God, sometimes as complaint, almost always as petition. The presence of these and similar qualities in more than fifty psalms has led many people to call them lament psalms, an analogy to lamentation over someone's death.

By the end of this unit most students find themselves deeply engaged in issues that range from the experiential (personal prayer in times of anger) to the theological (what kind of God can we address in anger?). These classes demonstrate that psalms of lament have a powerful effect on people, and in a group study they educate for the entire psalter.

STRUCTURE OF LAMENT PSALMS

Psalm 13 provides a straightforward illustration of the structure of lament psalms.

To the leader. A Psalm of David.

1   How long, O LORD? Will you forget me forever?
    How long will you hide your face from me?

2   How long must I bear pain in my soul,
        and have sorrow in my heart all day long?
    How long shall my enemy be exalted over me?
3   Consider and answer me, O LORD, my God!
        Give light to my eyes, or I will sleep the sleep
        of death,
4   and my enemy will say, "I have prevailed";
        my foes will rejoice because I am shaken.
5   But I trusted in your steadfast love;
        my heart shall rejoice in your salvation.
6   I will sing to the LORD,
        because he has dealt bountifully with me.

Almost all the typical elements of a lament psalm appear in this psalm.

Addressing God: "O LORD" (v. 1).

Complaining/lamenting the distress: plaintive words: "why?" "how long?" (three times in v. 1)

——against *human enemies*: "How long shall my enemy be exalted over me?" (v. 2c); worried that "my enemy will say, 'I have prevailed,' my foes will rejoice" (v. 4).

——against *God (as enemy)*: "How long, LORD? Will you forget me forever? How long will you hide your face from me?" (v. 1)

——about *self as enemy* (personal experience of worthlessness, feelings of depression): "How long must I bear pain in my soul, and have sorrow in my heart all day long?" (v. 2)

Professing innocence or confessing sins that bring suffering: Some psalms contain admissions of guilt and pleas for deliverance, while others complain that evil comes in spite of the psalmist's innocence (see Job 3, 7). In Psalm 13 this issue does not arise.

Petition for what one desires from God (often commands,

issued in imperatives): "Consider and answer me, O LORD, my God! Give light to my eyes or I will sleep the sleep of death" (v. 3).

Confession of trust in God who has saved us before (begins with words like *still, nevertheless*): "But I trusted in your steadfast love" (v. 5a).

Word of salvation (very seldom found in psalms).

Vowing to praise God (occasionally promising thanksgiving sacrifice): "I will sing to the LORD because he has dealt bountifully with me" (v. 6). Many lament psalms contain several of the elements described above, but not all of them.

Since the deepest reasons for lamenting emerge from the language used by the psalmist, reading these psalms carefully reveals the kinds of problems brought to God: sickness (Ps 6:2, 4, 7; Ps 38, 41); false accusations (Ps 7:3–5); malicious gossip (Ps 31:18); need for asylum (Ps 61:3–4); oppression (Ps 94:6, 16, 20–21); old age (Ps 71). Others do not indicate a clear reason for the psalmist's complaint, but the situation is clearly terrible. For example, Psalm 22, "My God, my God, why have you forsaken me?" reflects various complaints, but none stands out as central. This difficulty in identifying the root cause of suffering may reflect our experience; often it is hard to isolate the central issue from the others we experience. In this way laments reflect some of the tragic realities of our lives.

QUESTIONS TO ASK
WHEN READING A PSALM

Laments require us to listen carefully to the language of hurt and anger, to the descriptions of pain and frustration in the psalm. The following questions can assist us to reflect on our feelings and reactions to the language of lament: Who is the speaker? Who is being addressed? What is the mood? What does the psalmist desire? Again, Psalm 13 is our model.

The *speaker* bears pain and sorrow (v. 2), feels forgotten (v. 1), has been bested by an enemy (v. 2), and feels that death is imminent. The *addressee* in this psalm is God, named LORD in three places (vv. 1, 3, 6). The psalm's *mood* varies from impatience ("How long," v. 1) to sadness and anger (v. 2) to petulance (vv. 3–4), to cajoling ("but I trusted," "I will sing," vv. 5–6). The psalmist desires divine attention ("consider and answer me," v. 3) and a response, though the petition lacks concrete details. Notice how clearly the mood of the psalmist reflects the strained relationship between the addressee and the one addressed (God).

APPROPRIATING PSALMS FOR LIFE

DAVID AND THE PSALMS

The laments are found in a collection of psalms, not in stories that show how they could apply to everyday life. The Jewish compilers of the psalter realized that many people benefit from imagining a context for the psalms, so they added titles to some of them in order to situate the psalms in Israel's life. For example, Psalm 7 bears the title, "A lamentation of David, which he sang to the Lord concerning Cush, the Benjaminite" (ICEL 1994). No such story is known from the Bible, yet David surely was opposed by the tribe of Benjamin, both during and after the time of Saul; one can imagine that someone named Cush slandered David. Psalm 18 provides a second example: "A Psalm of David the servant of the LORD, who addressed the words of this song to the LORD on the day when the LORD delivered him from the hand of all his enemies, and from the hand of Saul." Here again the specifics are difficult to pinpoint, but it is not difficult for the reader of 1 and 2 Samuel to imagine such a scene. The most memorable of the titles is joined to Psalm 51: "A Psalm of David, when the prophet Nathan came to him, after he had gone in to Bathsheba." Most readers recall the story of David and Bathsheba, and Nathan's rebuke of David (2 Sam 11—12); imagining these events gives the psalm a life of its own. The reverse is also true. If one prays this psalm after hearing the story of David, Bathsheba, and Nathan, then one gets a sense of how to pray in similar situations. The Roman Catholic lectionary pairs these stories of David with Psalm 51, allowing the congregation to ponder the relationship between psalm and story.

In the Hebrew psalter eleven psalms contain titles that relate them to historical memories or events in the life of David: Psalms 3, 7, 30, 34, 51, 52, 54, 57, 59, 60, 102. The Greek translators of the psalms in the Septuagint continued the process. They added Davidic titles to an additional fourteen psalms beyond the seventy-four psalms ascribed to David's authorship in the Hebrew Masoretic text (Holladay 1993, 71). Three of these fourteen additional Davidic titles—Psalms 71, 96 and 97—relate to events or circumstances in his life.

These linkages show the yearning of Jewish worshipers to connect the life story of David, the reputed originator of the psalter, with various psalms. But not all people comfortably relate to the memory of David. Some might not imagine themselves as leaders, for example, or some women might yearn for experiences more directly related to their lives. Other biblical characters and stories broaden our horizon.

HANNAH AND LAMENTATION

Lament psalms undoubtedly had real-life settings. Some speculate that in early Israel one would have gone to a local shrine to beg God's intervention for serious need. The story of Hannah at the shrine of Shiloh (1 Sam 1—2) provides a fitting example. Her husband, Elkanah, went with her and his other wife, Peninah, at appointed times of the year. We learn from the story that Hannah suffered tremendous distress because she had no children, and Peninah mocked her. Hannah's experience of humiliation at the hand of her rival provides the basic *reason for lamentation*. She felt psychological suffering, which today we might describe as despair or depression. She "wept and would not eat" (1 Sam 1:8). Her husband could say or do nothing to relieve her anguish, so Hannah went before God: "She was deeply distressed and *prayed to the* LORD *and wept* bitterly" (1 Sam 1:10). As part of her prayer she vowed that if God would give her a son, she would dedicate him to God as a nazirite. Eli misunderstood her silent prayer and accused her of coming drunk to the shrine, so she felt mocked by yet another enemy. But Hannah protested her innocence: "I am a woman deeply troubled; I have drunk neither wine nor strong drink, but I have been pouring out my soul before the LORD." She begged him: "Do not regard your servant as a worthless woman, for I have been speaking out of my anxiety and vexation all this time" (1 Sam 1:15–16). She has made a petition to God, though not heard in the story, and also to Eli—Do not disregard me. This part of the story concludes with a remarkable change in the old priest, who responds: "Go in peace; the God of Israel grant the *petition* you have made to him" (1 Sam 1:17). This *word of salvation* leaves no cause to wonder why her mood changed when she returned with her husband.

This story helps us to imagine life settings of laments. One could vary the reasons considerably, but prayer to God with weeping and bitterness still fits the situation. In a Bible study on this story, the group once read Psalm 6, a lament psalm we already examined in chapter 1 for its poetic features. After hearing this psalm, a vigorous discussion began. One woman talked about Hannah praying this psalm, and others continued in the same vein, speaking of it as "her psalm." The point had been to hear it as a type of psalm appropriate to Hannah's story, but the group identified it as "hers." This psalm, most likely written by a man, took on life as a woman's psalm because the contemporary hearers empathized with Hannah's experience of suffering; they heard the psalm voicing the kind of prayer they thought appropriate for the situation. As with the stories of David, it is a small move from Hannah's story to our personal stories, which would also provide a venue for lamentation It is easy to imagine a myriad of oppressions and hostilities that could fit the mood of this psalm, some more appropriate to women, others to men.

HOW WE ADDRESS GOD IN LAMENTS

One reason people can identify with such psalms derives from the frank and concrete language they contain—especially the ways in which they address God—and how they help people to articulate their feelings. In Psalm 6 the speaker issues blunt orders to God: "Stop rebuking me, LORD, hold back your rage" (v. 2); "Repent, LORD, save me. You promised; keep faith" (v. 5). The speaker also complains to God: "LORD, how long, how long?" (v. 4), and we already have heard the complaint that God rebukes the psalmist, lets rage blaze away, and pulls back on divine promises. The psalmist's plea for life sounds like an attempt to bribe God: "In death, who remembers you? In Sheol, who gives you thanks?" (v. 6). As if God will miss our praise! But that is precisely the point: The lamenter believes intensely that God will miss one person's songs of praise, that this one person makes a difference to God. This language of lament bespeaks a bond, a personal relationship between the one who prays and the God of the covenant. Such language rests on faith and relies on personal and communal memories of God hearing the cry of the oppressed, the lamenter, the lowly—and answering that cry. In Hannah's story Eli announced God's hearing and intention to respond (oracle of salvation), but her feeling of assurance rests not only on the old priest's word but also on the solid rock of Israel's experience of God's long-lasting love. The people of Israel had regularly cried out to God ever since their suffering in Egypt and continually experienced God's saving intervention, beginning with their deliverance at the Reed Sea. Concrete stories feed the memory and allow worshipers in their time and ours to speak frankly, realistically, emotionally, and without fear of recrimination from God. A psalm that lacks such concrete charges against God, anger expressed toward God, probably has ceased to function as a lament.

To summarize: The rhetoric of lament in these psalms (Why? How long? Who else will praise you? How much?) permits us to engage similar rhetoric in our own prayer without fearing recrimination, condemnation, or even humiliation by others because we lament. These psalms not only permit us to express our anger against God, they also teach us words and ways in which to do so. The verbs and adjectives with which they describe and address God model for us open, honest biblical prayer of lamentation. They help us to learn *how* to articulate the pain and the grief that we experience; we don't have to internalize it, let it fester and grow sour. Laments lower the risk of venting anger in dangerous and inappropriate ways. When we can pray laments we acknowledge God's covenantal bond with us. Could we ever address a mere acquaintance or associate so directly without fear of reprisal or total abandonment? Can we afford not to pray psalms of lament in our day?

We have stressed the individual's prayer of lament, but the existence of the genre of communal lament lets us know that laments were the prayers of the community on occasion of great need. In the next chapter we will discuss communal laments and the issues that they and other lament psalms raise for contemporary praying communities.

PRAYING LAMENT PSALMS

No less now than in the past, God desires to hear our pain. Praying the psalms of lament provides us with both a tutorial and a vehicle for expressing our pain directly to God. Choose psalms that are meaningful to your prayer at a given moment. Remain with a psalm for as long as it is fruitful. You may wish to select one or several of the following psalms of individual lament for your prayer: Psalms 3, 4, 5, 7, 13, 17, 22, 31, 35, 42—43, 55, 57, 59, 69, 71, 88, or 109. Additional psalms of individual lament are listed in Appendix 1, "Psalms by Type."

LECTIO DIVINA WITH LAMENT PSALMS

• Review the general description of *lectio divina* in chapter 2 until you are familiar with the movements and do not need the directions.

• Select a lament psalm listed above, or another to which you feel drawn.

• Allow the movements of *lectio divina* to flow in and out of each other for as long as they are lively or for the length of time that you have set aside for prayer.

• At the conclusion of the *lectio divina* period, note in your journal what happened—for example, the word or phrase(s) you focused on, some of the ruminations or insights that came to you, the core of your response of God, and the tone of the contemplative moment.

• You may wish to return to the same psalm at a second prayer session, allowing the repetition to carry you deeper in the same direction or into a new place in the same psalm. Journal as above. Repeat as long as the psalm still contains "energy" or until you feel finished. You may use a single psalm three or more times. There is no need to cover all the psalms suggested.

HANDMADE MIDRASH

• Review the commentary on the psalm you have chosen. Reflect on the psalm (perhaps through *lectio divina*) and select the essence that you will express visually.

• Using pen or pencil on white paper, express this essence. Do not try to make representational figures (figures that obviously portray someone or something). Allow the marks to come uncensored from the point of the pen or pencil.

• Discuss your drawing with one other person. Ask what he or she sees in your visual expression of this psalm. You might also note which forms were the hardest and easiest to express. Other helpful questions are found in chapter 2.

• Write in your journal. The many possibilities to explore in writing might include free association, allowing new or unsettling thoughts to surface and be expressed.

• Reflect: How does the psalm now speak to or for you?

EXPRESSING PSALMS IN MOVEMENT

• Are there specific postures named in the psalm you have selected? As you read it aloud (or hear it on tape), make these movements and take these postures. You may wish to act out several characters: God, the psalmist, nature, armies, and so on.

• Alternatively, express the psalm through free movement. Express not only the movement words of your psalms but the feeling words as well. For example, how might you express in movement "I am weary with crying out, my throat is parched"?

• Write about what was evoked in you through this expressive movement.

WRITING YOUR OWN PSALM OF LAMENT

• Think of a situation in which lament is the most appropriate response. It may be your own experience, that of a community to which you belong, or the situation of an individual or community you know only indirectly yet empathize with. Now, write your own lament in the style of a psalm. Before you begin, you might wish to reread Psalm 6 or 13 as an example.

SINGING THE PSALMS

• Select a lament psalm known to you and sing it several times, until it has impressed itself upon you. Try to memorize a portion of the psalm in this musical setting and sing it (interiorly or aloud) throughout the day. On another day select another lament psalm setting and repeat the process. You may choose from the following short list of laments (the full titles of the hymnals are in the list of abbreviations in the front of the book). You may

also find other lament psalm hymns from your own tradition's hymnals.

Psalm Hymns of Individual Lament

Psalm	Title	Tune/Composer	Hymnal
13	How Long, O Lord	Schutte	G&P
22	Lord, Why Have You Forgotten Me?	Conditor Alme Siderum	PH
22	My God, My God	Haugen	G
27	Remember Your Mercies	Haas	G
27	Remember Your Love	Ducote/Daigle	G, G&P
31	I Put My Life in Your Hands	Haugen	G
39	O Lord, Hear My Prayer	Berthier (Taizé)	G
42	As Pants the Hart for Cooling Streams	Martyrdom CM	LBW, HEC, NCH
51	*Parce Domine*	Parce Domine	W, G
61	Be Thou My Vision	Slane	most hymnals
102	O Lord, Hear My Prayer	Berthier (Taizé)	G
130	Out of the Depths	Aus Tiefer Not	PH, UMH, HEC, LBW

CORPORATE PSALM PRAYER:
CRYING OUT TO GOD IN OUR NEED

• Pray the following service based on Evening Prayer. For
background on this form of prayer, see chapter 2. You may
wish to sing the psalms for which music is available. You
are encouraged to select hymns, antiphons, and psalm settings from your community's worship and hymn tradition.

Service of Light
    Greeting: Light and peace in Jesus Christ our Lord.
    Thanks be to God.
    Poem of Light: Rainer Maria Rilke

Lament

Oh, everything is far
and long ago.
I believe that star
these thousand years is dead,
though I see its light.
I believe, in that boat
passing through the night
something fearful was said.
In the house a clock
struck...
Where did it strike?...
I would like to walk
out of my heart under the wide sky.
I would like to pray.
One of all these stars
must still exist.
I believe I know
which one still lasts
and stands like a city, white
in the sky at the end of the beam of light.

Psalm 42—43 (sung or recited antiphonally)

Psalm Prayer
    O God, you are the fountain of generous life. Through the waters of baptism you called us to the depths of your mercy. From the refreshing springs of your Word satisfy our thirst for you, that we may come rejoicing to your holy mountain, where you live and reign now and forever. **Amen.**

Psalm 137 (sung or recited antiphonally)

Psalm Prayer
> O God, we sit weeping at the streams of Babylon. Stretch out your hand to us, strengthen in us the work of your love and bring us to new life. **Amen.**

Reading: Jeremiah 20:10–13

Silent Reflection (or brief homily)

Gospel Canticle: Canticle of Mary (may be sung or recited in unison)

Intercessory Prayers: To all prayers, respond: **Lord, have mercy.**

The Lord's Prayer

Concluding Prayer
> O God, holy is your name, and everlasting your compassion, cherished by every generation. Hear our evening prayer and let us sing your praise and proclaim the greatness of your mercy forever. We ask this through Jesus Christ, your Son, who lives and reigns with you and the Holy Spirit, one God forever and ever. **Amen.**
>
> May the Lord bless us, protect us from all evil and bring us to everlasting life. **Amen.**

Note: As you become familiar with the various prayer forms that lend themselves to praying with the psalms, you may wish to mix these prayer forms freely, as the Holy Spirit leads you. For example, handmade midrash may be a natural outgrowth of the *oratio* moment of *lectio divina*.

Psalm 137

1 By the rivers of Babylon—
   there we sat down and there we wept
   when we remembered Zion.
2 On the willows there
   we hung up our harps.
3 For there our captors
   asked us for songs,
  and our tormentors asked for mirth, saying,
   "Sing us one of the songs of Zion!"

4 How could we sing the LORD's song
   in a foreign land?
5 If I forget you, O Jerusalem,
   let my right hand wither!
6 Let my tongue cling to the roof of my mouth,
   if I do not remember you,
  if I do not set Jerusalem
   above my highest joy.

7 Remember, O LORD, against the Edomites
   the day of Jerusalem's fall,
  how they said, "Tear it down! Tear it down!
   Down to its foundations."
8 O daughter Babylon, you devastator!
   Happy shall they be who pay you back
   what you have done to us!
9 Happy shall they be who take your little ones
   and dash them against the rock!

Four

Crying Out to God in Need: Lament Psalms for the Community

Since all people suffer setbacks and losses at some point in their lives, we frequently hear expressions of relief when they discover lament psalms. Lamenting offers a prayerful way forward in these crisis times. Despite this frequent response, laments have been all but banished from our common liturgical prayer. What has happened? What consequences flow from this situation?

The following account illustrates the problem. The setting is a seminary class in pastoral spirituality, with students from a variety of denominations all approaching the conclusion of their studies and the beginning of various ministries and pastorates. We had been examining corporate psalm prayer as a resource for congregational spirituality. A gentle, second-career student, whose background included conscientious objection and other nonviolent lifestyle choices, declared forcefully, "When I am ordained and pastor my own church, I will never use the psalms in worship, in any form, at any time!" The class lapsed into stunned silence. "But you can't just excise a whole biblical book from worship," someone stammered.

"But I will," he returned. "I will not have the violence and all that military imagery before my congregation, let alone in its worship. It isn't Christian!"

While this student was very blunt and forceful in his objection to psalms as a resource for worship and communal spirituality, many others share his discomfort. A significant and telling precedent for excluding psalms from public worship appeared in John Wesley's *The Sunday Service of the Methodists in North American. With Other Occasional Services* (1784). In a study of the use of lament psalms in the 1989 *United Methodist Hymnal* Gaye Benson notes: "Wesley omitted thirty-four psalms completely and edited others severely, labeling them 'highly improper for the mouths of a Christian Congregation.'" The 1989 hymnal, while giving the psalms a more prominent place than did Wesley, still includes only one-hundred psalms. Laments constitute the greatest number of omissions (Benson 1995, 1–2).

Lament as a mood, and lament psalms in particular, have virtually disappeared from the official worship texts of the major Christian churches. The psalters published within official worship resources routinely omit the so-called imprecatory psalms, as does the Roman Catholic *Liturgy of the Hours*. The psalms retained are often "sanitized" by excising verses considered offensive to modern sensibilities. For example, Psalm 139 regularly loses verses 19–22:

> 19 If only you would destroy the wicked, O God,
>   and the bloodthirsty would depart from me!
> 20 Deceitfully they invoke your name;
>   your foes swear faithless oaths.
> 21 Do I not hate, LORD, those who hate you?
>   Those who rise against you, do I not loathe?

> 22 With fierce hatred I hate them,
>   enemies I count as my own. (RNAB)

Then the psalmist continues (and we resume our truncated reading):

> 23 Probe me, God, know my heart;
>   try me, know my concern.
> 24 See if my way is crooked,
>   then lead me in the ancient paths. (RNAB)

We are blissfully unaware that, in fact, we may stand to be judged for our hatred, revenge, factionalism, and judgmentalism as well as our righteous anger, patience, lovingkindness, prayerfulness, and praise invoked earlier in the psalm.

But the praying community also needs modes of lament, just as individuals do. How do we give permission for those in the community—for the community itself—to rage and weep? How do we call the community past a self-satisfied sense that "God is in heaven, and all is right with the world?" How do we invite the community to passionate engagement with the pain of creation? How do we bring to prayer concrete and specific situations of injustice? How do we reveal to ourselves and to God the web of violence in which we are enmeshed? How do we begin to respond when the situation is too big, too awful to imagine, let alone to work against? The lament psalms and other forms of lament may hold the clue.

Psalm prayer enters into the way things are but often finds that the way things are is pretty bad. We do encounter evil and injustice, both individually and on a massive scale. Psalm prayer, says Eugene Peterson, can be combat, and it is not for those looking for spiritual soporifics (1989, 95). They quickly give up praying the psalms. But when we rage, when our adrenalin flows, when we get excited, we may shout, wail, and weep. All this is present in the psalms. There was no shortage then, nor is there now, of desperate situations in which individuals and communities come face to face with such pain that they must cry out to God for vindication.

Psalms of lament move beyond the lament of one individual's situation; they also invite us to focus on the suffering, pain, and oppression of people throughout the world. Some laments clearly refer to situations affecting groups. These psalms are called *communal laments*. Communal laments reveal a world of natural pestilence (Joel 1—2) or military danger and defeat, especially the wrenching experiences of lost battles and the desecration of Jerusalem and the Temple (Pss 44, 74, 79, 80, 85). These psalms may heighten our awareness of human suffering in our world. Unjust and oppressive social structures and governments have led to a frightening level of oppression, hostility, and enmity that many people feel. Lament psalms can help us attend to our world's ills.

Even when not personally feeling a need to lament— and consequently perhaps alienated by a lament psalm in public prayer—these psalms still invite us to join in the experience, feelings, and prayers of others who suffer terribly. A good example of this is the woman who identified with the feelings of Hannah and could recognize Psalm 6 as "her" psalm. Lament psalms can raise our empathy and compassion for many individuals and groups suffering today. We might lament with indigenous peoples, victims of violence, civilians caught in civil wars, persons with AIDS or other life-threatening diseases, the poor, or victims of abuse. Once a person has allowed an imaginative presence of a suffering person or group to surface, then the psalm can be prayed with and for them. Many people have written their own "laments" about the world; some are poetic, others take the form of letters or essays about social ills ranging from racism to street violence to the death penalty. These people embody Paul VI's observation: "The person who prays the psalms prays not so much in his own person as in the name of the Church, and, in fact, in the person of Christ himself" (1975, 58).

But the psalms themselves invite their expression in public worship. Not only does the collection contain individual laments to be prayed in solidarity by contemporary individuals, it also contains communal laments to be prayed *by the community* when it is in distress. Probing these communal laments may help us reclaim lament in our corporate liturgical prayer.

THE LAMENT OF THE EXILES IN BABYLON

The realities that brought the community of Israel to its knees were not surprising: military foes about to overwhelm them, pestilence, famine, or drought. Only one lament psalm has so clear a reference that its location is unmistakable: Psalm 137 is clearly prayed from Babylon, a beautiful, sorrowful song that most feel is ruined by verse 9. Yet, if you have lost, through no fault of your own, all your land, livelihood, security, family, your very identity as a people, and you are condemned to live out your existence in a refugee camp, full of hopelessness, why wouldn't such rage pour forth spontaneously? And who better to pour out rage to than the God who can honor it?

Let us look more closely at Psalm 137, cited at the beginning of this chapter. First, it is important to recognize the situation of the community as it prayed this psalm. The people themselves were in no position to dash the heads of their captors' children against the rock; in fact, they were helpless. They were desperately attempting to cling to their historical identity even when everything was against them. Even more significantly, in the face of their profound powerlessness, they were striving to rein in the violence in their own hearts by surrendering everything to God, even their desire for revenge.

In the first part of the psalm, verses 1–6, those who pray lament their own internal conflict. Their tormentors mock them by asking them to sing one of the songs of Zion, but they find it impossible to sing a song proclaiming God's power to save them while they are enslaved. They probably experience profound doubt about God's power to save them. The status quo contradicts the truth about God that they had believed and hoped for. In this crisis of faith they come to the conclusion that it is their *situation* that must be untenable, if indeed God remains their protector. Verses 1–6 expose their struggle, yet they renew their oath to place Jerusalem—and God—ahead of their doubt.

The second half of the psalm appeals to God to restore the rule of justice and order upon which their faith and the very nature of God rests. The language and images spring from the *lex talionis*, the retribution required to restore justice and end the violence once and for all. "Little ones" refers to the progeny of the royal house; verse 9 means, therefore, "destroy the dynasty that has wreaked such injustice."

Psalm 137 is a political poem, and it is important to hold both the political and the poetic in tension. As a poem, its work is done by means of the images, not by a literal enacting of the text. As a political statement, it addresses the arrangement of power and powerlessness experienced by the people and calls for the end of Babylon's reign of terror. Ironically, it is also a love poem, because only those who love can be so upset by the apparent betrayal of the passionate love between God and the people. Without verses 8–9, those excised in most Christian worship, we lose a key to a theologically acceptable understanding of its perspective on violence (Zenger 1996, 48–50).

Refugees throughout the world are estimated to be in the millions. Psalm 137—and other psalms of lament—can be prayed on behalf of all who suffer, in this case, refugees. Someone in the community is in grief, consumed with anger, hatred, revenge. Some communities are struggling for their very existence. Lament psalms offer us one way to stand in solidarity with our brothers and sisters, praying with them, or even in their stead when they are unable to pray.

Since all humans at some time or another experience suffering, lament psalms can allow us to move back and forth between our own suffering and that of others. Thus, Psalm 137, the lament of the homesick Jews in exile in Babylon, can also serve as a personal cry of despair and longing in our own time and place (Eilberg 1994, 91). Our own disorientation and loss unite with the disorientation and loss of those early exiles and with all those today in a similar predicament.

Most lament psalms, however, lack reference to concrete historical situations. They expressed the distress of the community in any number of situations when it was difficult for the people to believe that God was with them. Psalms without reference to specific situations had the virtue of being interchangeable; likewise, particular psalms could be employed for many types of crisis. Times without security, times relying on faith in the not-yet-seen work of God, times between God's promise and its fulfillment—these times elicit lament now as surely as then.

CAN RELIGIOUS PEOPLE CURSE THEIR ENEMIES?

What about language of vengeance? Let Psalm 69 serve as a test case for dealing with this significant pastoral issue. The cry for vindication, the tone of anger, and the desire for vengeance are in full swing in this psalm, especially in verses 22–29:

22 Let their table be a trap for them,
   a snare for their allies.
23 Let their eyes be darkened so that they cannot
   see,
   and make their loins tremble continually.
24 Pour out your indignation upon them,
   and let your burning anger overtake them.
25 May their camp be a desolation;
   let no one live in their tents.
26 For they persecute those whom you have struck
   down,
   and those whom you have wounded, they
   attack still more.
27 Add guilt to their guilt;
   may they have no acquittal from you.
28 Let them be blotted out of the book of the living;
   let them not be enrolled among the righteous.
29 But I am lowly and in pain;
   let your salvation, O God, protect me.

Other aspects of the lament psalm genre are more muted in Psalm 69. The psalmist is mired in the early stages of extreme distress, where hope is but a distant and faint possibility. All the psalmist is able to muster is a stick to beat on God with. The "hope" we get is hope in anticipation and in bargaining—not hope in full flower at all.

But that is also part of human experience. Who has been lucky enough to escape at least one bitterly hurtful experience carried around inside like a livid bruise to the spirit? How exquisitely painful when the wound is inflicted by a loved person, the church community, or by those with whom you minister, from whom you least expect an attack. Who among us hasn't said, if only to ourselves, "If I could just get my hands on him, I'd kill him!" The psalmist shouts to God: "Let them be blotted out of the book of the living!" (v. 28a).

This difficult psalm elicits still another question: Isn't the church wise to edit out this raw emotion from its worship? Not at all. We have, in fact, sold ourselves short using this strategy. In our desire to make worship palatable, we give people the impression that only positive prayers and loving thoughts and actions are appropriate for Christians. We have failed to model in our prayer the raw rage and anger that erupt in everyone at one time or other. We have not mirrored the range of persons in the worshiping community. On any given Sunday some people in the congregation leave convinced that their raw emotions are unacceptable and have no place in church. It may be a long time before they can return to worship with the community.

But the censoring of such raw emotion from our prayer has far greater implications than the faith and prayer of individual believers. Anger and rage unacknowledged go underground, not just in individuals, but in whole families, communities, nations, churches, where it wreaks havoc dissociated from its original cause. Displaced anger is far more dangerous than recognized and expressed anger. It can easily masquerade as righteousness, purity, the true faith, pure doctrine, and in this guise is almost impossible to touch, lance, and heal. Whole communities and nations are at war, each side certain that it is justified in its violent stance toward the other. If we lose—or never learn—the practice of unrestrained expression of rage in prayer, the sad corollary may be that we also lose the understanding that vengeance belongs only to God. Our individual and societal actions show that we desperately need to learn about anger and what to do with it. The psalms teach us to tell the whole of our story to God, self, and community (Craven 1992, 53–54; Wolff 1979, 57–58).

What, then, can we do with such raw anger and rage? Two things, perhaps. The first strategy, the preferred Orthodox method, understands the enemy in mythic terms; that is, the enemy stands for all the powers of darkness arrayed against us, stronger and more devious than we can hope to survive. Praying the lament psalms, then, becomes joining the cosmic battle against evil and arraying ourselves on God's side—cheering for God, as it were—in this combat for the heart of creation. A similar genre, the African American spiritual, emerged closer to our own time and place.

The second strategy is perhaps more immediately engaging and threatening: In the lament, we can throw all our rage at God's feet and not at the face of those with whom we are enraged. Or, perhaps more commonly for those of us raised to "be good," we can rage in the open instead of raging unconsciously. Those unconscious rages not only destroy us from the inside, but they come out in displaced form and destroy others who are often inappropriate targets. Acknowledging our rage can then begin the transformation offered by Jesus: "You have heard that it was said, 'You shall love your neighbor and hate your enemy.' But I say to you, Love your enemies and pray for those who persecute you, so that you may be children of your Father in heaven" (Matt 5:43–45a). Paul also speaks of the transformation and healing of our rage: "Bless those who persecute you; bless and do not curse them" (Rom 12:14). A long journey of grace occurs before this behavior flows from a truly healed and transformed heart. Until we acknowledge individually and corporately before God that we have such rage, we may not allow ourselves to receive God's transformative grace in Christ and to embrace Jesus' ethic of love of enemies. The cursing psalms can bring us face to face with the depth of our neediness before God.

A Roman Catholic sister from South Africa tells this personal story: She was facing a meeting with her religious superior, which she expected to be more of a confrontation than a conversation. The superior's decisions had placed this sister in an untenable position with respect to her ministry. She was angry and hurt and felt like lashing out at the woman who represented legitimate authority for her, an authority that seemed much more dominating than the word of God. It so happened that Evening Prayer contained one of the "cursing psalms." "I remember," she said, "how good it felt to hear those curses. Somebody knew what I felt like. But later, I realized I no longer needed to attack the superior, to defend myself and my ministry. I knew that God was in charge, and that God would deal with the situation in some way that might surprise both of us. I was able to let go of some of my anger, enough to approach the meeting with equilibrium, even hope. While all was not resolved in this meeting, it will be possible to continue meeting and exploring our differing perspectives on the situation. And we will be able to do this without becoming enemies."

Occasionally a church community does provide for communal lament. The services following the bombing of the Federal Building in Oklahoma City and the memorials for the victims of the Columbine High School shootings immediately come to mind. Such community laments allow for communal expression of pain and anguish in a context of faith and begin the long process of coming to terms with the horror. The Jubilee Year provided opportunities for churches and their leaders to express sorrow and to ask for forgiveness for wrongs committed by their members or through their policies. In one such service Bishop John Cummins of the Roman Catholic Diocese of Oakland asked forgiveness from victims of sexual abuse within church settings and thereby allowed the victims to lament their pain and suffering in worship. Many of those present expressed relief that their pain had been publicly acknowledged at last.

But there is still another troubling question. Even if we leave vengeance to God, what kind of God is this? The question jumps out of the first verse of Psalm 94: "O Lord, you God of vengeance, you God of vengeance, shine forth!"

Several exegetical points can help here. First, the more dynamic and accurate translations convey God's *activity* rather than God's essence. The revised psalms of the New American Bible have a better rendering: "LORD, avenging God, avenging God, shine forth!" The psalmist is not stating something about God's nature but something about God's actions: God is avenging the wronged. Second, God is not taking *revenge* (the commonly assumed meaning of the English word) but is restoring the damaged order of law. At stake is the action of the legally constituted authority making decisions according to legal principles to protect and advance the common good—precisely the opposite of what the English translations generally convey (Zenger 1996, 70–71).

One more crucial insight will assist in interpreting the picture of God in the so-called psalms of imprecation. This insight revolves around the quality of the relationship between the people and their God. Zenger claims: "The appeal and trust of those praying, in fact, depends essentially on the presupposition that God is *personally* touched by injustice, and is even called into question by it—and that God must bring about justice 'for the sake of God's own name'" (1996, 71). Thus, God is not an impartial arbitrator, judging the fine points of the case of one petitioner against another in carefully objective fashion. The psalmist knows that the living God is passionately involved with the people, who may then importune God to judge according to the terms of this covenant. The people may—indeed *must*—insist that God uphold justice and righteousness. One prays this prayer at one's own risk, hence the pleas of innocence. Justice is as required of the psalmist and the community as it is of God.

John Brook elegantly summarizes the purpose and fruit of laments as the community's prayer when he writes:

> The psalms of lament put us in the same situation for prayer as the psalms of praise. [When] we are in trouble, they can enable us to express our anguish, our cry to God. They give us words at times when words fail us. They can slowly winch us out of the pit. But what if we are joyful, and do not feel like praying a lament? Again, as with the psalms of praise, we can pray the lament as part of the body of Christ, entering into the experience of [some community that] is in despair, [some community whose] experience the words of the psalm describe. It is one way we can "weep with those who weep" (Rom 12:15). In praying the laments we can pray with people throughout the world who are suffering for their faith, or suffering because of injustice and greed of the rich and the powerful. (Brook 1992, 49)

But how do we answer the objection that the sentiments of these psalms are not Christian? We know Jesus prayed laments. They are on his lips twice during the passion: the familiar "My God, my God, why have you forsaken me?" of Psalm 22:1 and "Into your hand I commit my spirit" of Psalm 31:5. Thus, in imitation of Jesus, the Christian community has joined the long tradition of laments. We too live in the time between the hearing of the promise and its keeping. We too, following Jesus, can pray the laments with as much feeling as our ancient forbears.

PRAYING LAMENTS

We can find in communal laments powerful expressions of prayer both for ourselves and on behalf of others—in fact, these psalms can encourage us to imagine the circumstances of and stand in solidarity with others less fortunate than ourselves. Communal laments lend themselves to all the ways of personal prayer so far introduced: *lectio divina*, hymn singing, handmade midrash, movement prayer, writing personal psalms, and so on. The following communal laments may offer much fruit for personal prayer: Psalms 44, 60, 74, 77, 79, 80, 85, 90, and Lamentations 5. The "hard psalms" can challenge some aspect of our thinking, praying, or relating to others: Psalms 58, 69, 88, 109, and 137. The graces they offer are well worth struggling with the resistance we may initially experience at their language, images, and sentiments.

The following suggestions for prayer focus on the praying community, inviting it to return to the corporate practice of lament. Community lament prayer may arouse significant resistance, especially since present liturgical practice has not encouraged communities to struggle with the difficult sentiments that lament psalms embody. Yet communities inevitably face moments in which lament is singularly appropriate: times of national or community threat, loss of a beloved community member, significant times of illness or economic hardship, and closure of a ministry, for example.

GUIDED MEDITATION: ARTICULATING THE LAMENTS OF THE WORLD AND ITS PEOPLE

This prayer follows the form of lament psalms, namely, addressing God, articulating the complaint, professing innocence, stating the petition, confessing trust, and vowing to praise God again. It is presented here for use by small or large groups, but it also offers individuals a form for lament. If the group is small, all the movements can be articulated aloud by each participant, with each person interceding for a different painful situation. Alternatively, the entire group can lament over the same situation. Logistically, this option is particularly useful with a large group, where numbers will preclude sharing about a wide variety of lamentable situations. Apart from logistical considerations, when something tragic has occurred within a particular community, or upon such anniversaries as the first atomic bomb or World AIDS Day, group lament can be singularly appropriate. The leader should adapt the following steps in language suitable to the particular group assembled.

1. Formulating the Issue and Identifying with the Oppressed

• Begin by recalling a painful situation, a situation of injustice, a situation where others are under severe duress, some structural and intractable evil....Let God speak deeply within you to surface a condition which needs to be rectified and for which you will intercede.
• Be in touch with the variety and depth of the woundedness and estrangement evoked by this situation....Identify

as clearly as you are able with those caught in this situation....Name this situation aloud, so that all present may join in interceding.

2. Address to God

• Address God in whatever way seems fitting, calling God to hear you....Articulate your complaint forcefully, repeatedly, as strongly as you can.

3. Confession

• Our God is a God of compassion. Confess your trust in God in whatever words come to you....Place your petitions—yes, even your demands—before this God.

4. Words of Assurance

• Hear God speak words of assurance to you....Address words of assurance to yourself, to the community....Offer God your promise of praise in the face of this stubborn situation.

5. Conclusion

• Offer some group expression such as a hymn or sign of peace as the pastoral situation dictates.

LECTIO DIVINA IN COMMUNAL LAMENT

*Directions for the leader appear in parentheses
(Dreitcer 1997).*

(Select the lament text that the group will pray. Have the group members prepare themselves for prayer in whatever way is beneficial for them, or lead them in communal preparation, which may include recalling the painful or unjust situations evoking lament.)

1. (Invite the group to listen for a word or phrase that stands out or attracts them. Then read the passage twice,

the first time unhurriedly, the second time more slowly. Before the second reading, give the following directions:)
• Listen for a word or phrase that beckons, "shimmers," addresses you, stirs you, unnerves you, disturbs you. Repeat this word to yourself *(ruminatio)*. When the leader asks, share your word or phrase with the group. The leader should allow generous time between speakers. (The group may agree to take turns around the circle, with each person indicating to the next through a gesture, a touch, or a word that he or she is finished.)

2. (Invite the group to notice what feeling or image arises in them in relation to the word or phrase that has touched them. Then the passage is read aloud, preferably by a second person.)
• Attend to the feeling or image in you that is connected to the word or phrase you have spoken *(ruminatio* and *meditatio)*. Briefly state this feeling or image. (Use the same process as in the first sharing.)

3. (Invite the group members to consider their present situation and how what they have heard, felt, or noticed relates to their own life. Let them know they will have a certain amount of time to explore this before sharing it in the group. The passage is read a final time, perhaps by a third person.)
• Attend to the way this word or phrase, feeling, or image connects with the context and situation of your life right now. How does it relate to what you have heard and seen this day? How does it connect with what is happening at home, at work, in your leisure time? Take an extended time of exploring this connection (in thought, in a journal, in art, in movement). How is God present to you there? What is God like for you in your life? Is God calling you to anything in your present circumstance *(meditatio)*?
• Address your response to God in whatever way seems appropriate *(oratio)*. You may express this response in

your heart, in your journal, through some artistic medium, through movement.
• Briefly share with the group what you have discovered.
4. (Invite the group to a time of silent contemplation, a time of simply resting with and receiving what God has offered them [contemplatio]).
5. (Invite the group to address God directly in simple prayer [oratio]).
6. (Close with a spoken blessing or prayer.)

LITURGICAL LAMENT

Tenebrae services offer a powerful psalm-based communal lament service, yet few Christians in recent years have experienced it. *Tenebrae* means "shadows" or "darkness"; it evokes the setting of the Sun of Justice recalled during the Easter Tridiuum. Tenebrae replaces the readings and psalms of Matins and Lauds for Good Friday and Holy Saturday, each anticipated on the evening preceding. Prior to the 1956 reform of the Holy Week liturgy, Matins contained nine readings and nine psalms, and Lauds contained five psalms; Tenebrae thus consisted of fourteen psalms. Fifteen candles were lit at the beginning of the service and extinguished one by one at the end of each psalm to evoke the abandoning of Christ by the apostles. The unrecognized Light of Christ, represented by the fifteenth candle, was not destroyed. After being briefly placed on the altar or communion table, it was hidden and the church filled with a confusion of sounds, representing the travail of nature at the death of Christ. The light then reappeared—Christ is risen, and death is conquered (Lang 1989, 608–9).

The traditional psalms and readings for Tenebrae follow. (Note that the first number of the psalm is the Septuagint, Greek and Latin numbering used in older Roman Catholic versions; the second number is the way the psalm is listed in contemporary translations.) Varying the style of singing and/or reciting the psalms and dividing the readings among several voices add to the texture of the service. If Tenebrae is held only one night, the psalms may be selected from the complete list; the reading from Lamentations is traditionally selected for this service.

Good Friday

Matins
1. Psalms 2, 21(22), 26(27), followed by the reading of Lamentations 2:8–15 and 3:1–9.
2. Psalms 37(38), 39(40), 53(54), followed by a reading from Augustine, *Treatise on the Psalms,* on Psalm 63:2 (or other appropriate selection).
3. Psalms 58(59), 87(88), 93(94), followed by the reading from Hebrews 4:11—5:10.

Lauds
Psalms 50(51), 142(143), 84(85), Canticle of Habakkuk (Hab 3:2–19), Ps 147:12–20.
(The Canticle of Zachary follows. Part of the hymn from Philippians 2, verses 8–10, may also be done. The presider continues, while the final candle is burning):

> We are Your children, Lord; look upon us. It was to save us that our Lord Jesus Christ did not hesitate to deliver Himself into the hands of sinners and undergo the torment of the Cross.

(All depart in silence.)

Holy Saturday

Matins
1. Psalms 4, 14(15), 15(16), followed by the reading of Lamentations 3:22–30, 4:1–6, 5:1–11.

2. Psalms 23(24), 26(27), 29(30), followed by a reading from Augustine, *Treatise on the Psalms,* on Ps 63:7 (or other suitable selection).
3. Psalms 53(54), 75(76), 87(88), followed by the reading of Hebrews 9:11–22.

Lauds
Psalms 50(51), 91(92), 63(64), Canticle of Hezekiah (Is 38:10–20), 150.
(The Canticle of Zachary follows. Part of the hymn from Philippians 2, verses 8–10, may also be done. The presider continues, while the final candle is burning:)

> In devout expectation we look forward to the resur-rection of Your Son, O God all-powerful. Grant that we may enjoy the glory of that resurrection.

(All depart in silence.)

EXPRESSING COMMUNAL LAMENTS VISUALLY

Visual expression of our response to situations of lament adds a powerful component to communal prayer. In one recent lament service for an inner-city neighborhood rav-aged by drugs, slides depicting the graffiti memorializing neighborhood youth killed in drug violence galvanized people to resist and reclaim the neighborhood. A small group might convene to develop a visual expression of lament, from a banner to the entire environment of the worship space—a liturgical arts committee would be ideal, but others, even without artistic skill, can participate in this form of prayer. This group should prayerfully probe the situation for which the community is lamenting and collectively decide upon the visual symbol. Group mem-bers may give suggestions to the person developing the art or layout and assist with the construction. This entire process can be seen as an embodied prayer producing a concrete expression in service of the larger community.

Prayer or retreat groups can employ handmade midrash, with each person expressing his or her response to the situation being lamented. These individual expressions may be shared, displayed, or carried in procession. The cumulative visual expression can evoke new levels of participation in corporate prayer.

PROCESSION

Because it involves the active participation of the praying community and takes seriously the location of events, procession can become a powerful form for lament services. Procession can be especially forceful for naming situations of oppression and violence in the local community.

Many celebratory psalms seem to have been composed particularly for procession, but they are more appropriate for processions of a different mode. Here lament psalms and selections from the Book of Lamentations provide the texts. The redemptive dimension of worship encourages participants to hope for and participate in their transformation and the transformation of the very situation evoking the lament. Including such texts as Lamentations 3:19ff., 31ff., 40ff., and 55ff. invites the worshipers to focus simultaneously on the past, present, and future within God's providence, judgment, and ultimately, salvation.

As a form, procession has almost unlimited variations. It may begin or end in a church or in a public space. An introductory rite and a concluding rite mark its beginning and end. Those processing may stop at predetermined places where they hear suitable scriptures followed by commentary or story and possibly experience a ritual action. As people move, simple hymns or litanies can unite the group; banners can focus not only the worshipers but also the onlookers (Henderson 1994, 20).

EXPRESSING COMMUNAL LAMENT PSALMS IN MOVEMENT

Psalm 137

• Select a hymn text to Psalm 137. Listen to this hymn repeatedly. Let the music penetrate your spirit. Together share the meaning of this psalm hymn, both in its original context and today, and develop some simple movements to express the essence of the psalm. Share the movements in an appropriate prayer context. Reflect together on the experience of corporate movement as an expression of your prayer and understanding.

Lamentations 5

• In a group, pray Lamentations 5 using *lectio divina*. At the conclusion of the process note the key words and images that arose in the group. Place these words and images in an order that feels appropriate. Develop motions to express each of these words and images. The person who shared the word or image may take the lead for this section, or the group may generate the movements together. When offered within a worship setting, ask one person to read the scripture text for the worshiping community, then offer the words/images and their expression in movement.

SINGING COMMUNAL LAMENT PSALMS

These hymns may be used in communal services of lament or, following the suggestions in the preceding chapter, for individual lament prayer. This short list of lament-oriented hymns may lead to others in your hymnal.

Psalm	Title	Tune/Composer	Hymnal
44	God of Our Fathers	National Hymn	NCH, W
85	Make Us Turn to You	Haugen	G
85	*Muéstranos Señor*	Cortez	G&P
90	O God, Our Help in Ages Past	St. Anne CM	most hymnals
126	Psalm 126	Gelineau	PC, G
137	By the Babylonian Rivers	Kas Dziedaja	PH, W, WOV

CORPORATE PSALM PRAYER IN A SITUATION OF VIOLENCE

Evening Prayer, with its more solemn tone and use of light and darkness, lends itself to lament situations. You may wish to sing the psalms for which music is available. (Many hymn texts omit whole sections of lament and may therefore change the tone; you may need to compensate for this omission.) The service that follows relies on prayers and litanies from *Liturgies of Lament* (Henderson 1994, 69–71, 73). The worshipers assemble in a darkened church or worship space. The service begins by the lighting of the Easter candle.

Service of Light
> *Greeting*: The light shines in the darkness. **And the darkness did not overcome it.**
> *Hymn*: traditionally "Phos Hilaron," an ancient hymn to Christ as Light

Prayer
> Blessed are you, Lord God of all creation. In the beginning you separated light from darkness and placed all your works in our hands. Break through the darkness of our sins with the splendor of your

mercy and love. Send your light to dispel our fears and anxieties and fill us with hope and joy. Through Christ Jesus our Lord, in the power of the Holy Spirit. **Amen.**

Evening Psalm (Psalm 141)

Psalm Prayer

Holy God, we pour out our hearts to you in complaint, yet we also lift up our hands to you in intercession. Hear our prayer. You alone can meet the deepest needs of our bodies and our spirits and make them whole again. This we ask through Christ our brother. **Amen.**

Psalm 79

Psalm Prayer

O God, you have promised us that you will dwell with us as our God, and that we will be your people. One day you will wipe every tear from our eyes, death will be no more, and mourning and crying and pain will be no more, for you make all things new. We praise you and long for the fullness of your reign, in Jesus Christ's name. **Amen.**

Scripture: Lamentations 3:19–24

Response

Jesus Christ, our brother and liberator, you have told us: Blessed are the poor in spirit, **for theirs is the kingdom of heaven.**

Blessed are those who mourn, **for they will be comforted.**

Blessed are the meek, **for they will inherit the earth.**

Blessed are those who hunger and thirst for righteousness, **for they will be filled.**

Blessed are the merciful, **for they shall obtain mercy.**

Blessed are the pure of heart, **for they will see God.**

Blessed are the peacemakers, **for they will be called children of God.**
Blessed are those who are persecuted for righteousness' sake, **for theirs is the kingdom of heaven.**
Blessed are you when people revile you and persecute you and utter all kinds of evil against you falsely on my account, **rejoice and be glad, for your reward is great in heaven.**
We praise you and we long for the fullness of God's reign. **Amen.**

Intercessions
Individual prayers are offered, each concluding with:
Lord, in your mercy, **Hear our prayer.**

The Lord's Prayer

Concluding Rites, Blessing, and Dismissal
May the God who heals us and our violent world bless us and be with us always. **Amen.**
Let us offer one another the sign of peace.

Psalm 30

1   *A psalm. A song for the dedication of the temple.*
    Of David.
    I
2   I praise you, LORD, for you raised me up
        and did not let my enemies rejoice over me.
3   O LORD, my God,
        I cried out to you and you healed me.
4   LORD, you brought me up from Sheol;
        you kept me from going down to the pit.

    II
5   Sing praise to the LORD, you faithful;
        give thanks to God's holy name.
6   For divine anger lasts but a moment;
        divine favor lasts a lifetime.
    At dusk weeping comes for the night;
        but at dawn there is rejoicing.

    III
7   Complacent, I once said,
        "I shall never be shaken."
8   LORD, when you showed me favor
        I stood like the mighty mountains.
    But when you hid your face
        I was struck with terror.
9   To you, LORD, I cried out;
        with the Lord I pleaded for mercy:
10 "What gain is there from my lifeblood,
        from my going down to the grave?
    Does dust give you thanks
        or declare your faithfulness?
11 Hear, O LORD, have mercy on me;
        LORD, be my helper."

12 You changed my mourning into dancing;
   you took off my sackcloth
   and clothed me with gladness.
13 With my whole being I sing
   endless praise to you.
   O LORD, my God,
   forever will I give you thanks. (RNAB)

Five
Thanking God Present and Active in Our Lives: Thanksgiving Psalms

"How I love a grateful heart!" This exclamation probably does not surprise any of us, for we intuitively recognize the joy of expressing gratitude. A person who is thankful usually exudes joy and receptivity, shares a message of surprising benefits, and contributes to a general feeling of goodness. Most of us appreciate someone who is thoughtful enough to thank us for a favor done or a courtesy offered. Those simple words—"thank you"—almost always build up a relationship between the person who is expressing gratitude and the one who experiences this gift. Clearly, persons possessed of thankful hearts experience both joy and the bonds of trusted relationship. They possess something far more important than a multitude of possessions.

Grateful hearts, however, don't simply describe happy, positive people. We focus not merely on a disposition, a lighthearted approach to life and other people. When we connect gratitude with certain persons, we do so because they can identify both pain and pleasure in their lives, hurt and healing, sadness and joy, anguish and salvation, hunger and satiety. They can also express each end of these polarities to God and to others; they can bring both their sadness and their joy to one another. This ability usually stems from a relationship, a bond of trust that allows people to express what they think and feel and desire, whether positive or negative.

We express genuine gratitude when we thank someone for something specific and then let it rest with no strings attached. We thank God for specifics, for ways that God answered our prayers, for occasions when God clearly heard our laments and responded to them. When God saved us from illness or rescued our loved ones from a disaster, we thank God. For a job received, or an enemy's power diminished, for a pregnancy long sought in prayer, like Hannah's, we thank God. When an injustice has finally been reversed, after a long time of petitioning and waiting, we thank God. For anything that we have brought with lament and its insistent petition to God, we offer thanks and gratitude. We express gratitude for particular gifts of God and others. We may use words of praise and thankfulness addressed to God but also said aloud so others may hear and join in our gratitude.

On some occasions people offer gifts to show their gratitude, perhaps a donation to the church or to some person or group in genuine need. Sometimes when we beg God for help of some kind, we make a promise to do something if our request is granted. In many societies this promise is called a vow, like the promise Hannah made that if God would give her a son she would dedicate him to God as a nazirite. In our day many parents tell of promises they made to God if their child would survive a terrible illness or injury. For all these people, giving a "gift" to God constitutes an important part of their giving thanks to God. People demonstrate their gratitude to God both by words and by actions.

Living with a grateful heart means that we live conscious of God's gifts to us. Experiencing God's goodness may lead to praise for God's creative and saving actions in our world. Thanksgiving, on the other hand, expresses best the hopes and feelings of people who have cried out to God in their distress and then have experienced God's saving intervention. They are conscious of specifics much more than generalities. They feel compelled to thank God for this particular favor, for an important grace that they or their loved ones experienced personally. Rather than focusing on the cosmic, as tends to happen in praise psalms, their concern is primarily with *this* time and *this* place.

THANKSGIVING AS A TYPE OF PSALM

Psalms used to express thanksgiving to God use a particular kind of language and often have an identifiable process or structure. To describe the similarities in these psalms we use the term *thanksgiving psalms*. These psalms often begin with a single person speaking words of thanks to God, and they often continue with some description of the trials and tribulations that led the person to beg God's help. This part of the psalm reminds one of the laments, even though it usually only mentions certain parts of the complaint and petition. Like the laments, this type includes both individual and communal psalms.

The tone of these psalms is joyous, and we who read and pray them sense that some wonderful deed of God caused this outburst of joy, even if we cannot precisely determine what happened. The important realization remains the clear sense of concrete goodness eliciting an acknowledgment of gratitude. Some of these psalms include a specific reference to a thanksgiving gift or sacrifice at the temple or a shrine. Finally, most of them repeat the desire to thank God joyfully.

STRUCTURE OF THANKSGIVING PSALMS

One of the best examples of a thanksgiving psalm is Psalm 30. This psalm includes typical elements that we can identify and describe. Psalm citations here are from RNAB.

Introduction: "I praise you, LORD" (v. 2a). Usually the introduction contains some word for thanking, praising, or rejoicing.

Reason for Thanking God: The psalmist tries to express the reasons for offering thanks to God. Often we can recognize this element in the psalm by the conjunction *for* or *because*, as in verse 2b: "for you raised me up and did not let my enemies rejoice over me." After this very general beginning the psalmist continues: "O LORD, my God, I cried out to you and you healed me. LORD, you brought me up from Sheol; you kept me from going down to the pit" (vv. 3–4). "Healed" informs us that the psalmist suffered from a very serious illness and was cured by God. "Sheol" describes the abode of the dead in Hebrew thought, so God snatched this person from the jaws of death. In some way the psalmist cried out to God, probably in a lament-like prayer, for we have here the typical language of lament: "cry out." But wonder of wonders, God answered! Not only did God respond, but the psalmist rejoices in renewed strength because of God's response. We do not know the details, but we do know that something really marvelous happened.

Note that in this particular psalm a second set of reasons to thank God follows the next part, the call to the community to thank God. This second set sounds much like the description of troubles and perils in a psalm of lament. Reading verses 7–12 of Psalm 30 reveals much more about the psalmist's personality and experience. This person had been living carelessly, complacently, assuming God's protection all the time. In times of grace the psalmist stood high and proud but was terrorized in times of trouble. As in many lament psalms, the psalmist not only begged God's help, but also provided motives for God to act: If I die, there will be one less person praising you. The petition is repeated (v. 11), and then the psalmist exclaims a second time how God had intervened (v. 12). The language of clothing gives a physical quality to the emotions the psalmist felt and may remind us of similar experiences and feelings. Even more, the sense of mourning turning to dancing conveys the transformation of the psalmist's experience and feelings.

Call to Thank God: After the first set of reasons for thanking God, the psalmist invites others to join in thanking God, now that they have heard this good news (vv. 5–6). This particular call to thanksgiving generalizes about God's anger and mercy from the present experience of healing as a reason for the congregation to participate in joyful gratitude.

5 Sing praise to the Lord, you faithful;
       give thanks to God's holy name.
6 For divine anger lasts but a moment;
       divine favor lasts a lifetime.
    At dusk weeping comes for the night;
       but at dawn there is rejoicing. (RNAB)

Praise and Thanks to God: At the conclusion of the psalm is a reiteration of the psalmist's intention to sing thanks to God. "With my whole being I sing endless praise to you. O LORD, my God, forever will I give you thanks."

Most psalms of thanksgiving contain these four elements, though not always in the same order or in the same proportion. Keys to recognizing thanksgiving psalms are words for thanks or praise and mention of the distress or illness that led the psalmist to cry out to God.

QUESTIONS WHEN READING THANKSGIVING PSALMS

Thanksgiving psalms bring to our attention the fluctuation of moods and fortunes, of emotions and life situations. When reading or hearing these psalms, we suggest the same set of preliminary questions as before. Who is the speaker? Whom does the psalmist address? What is the mood? What does the psalmist desire? What images of God characterize this psalm? Psalm 30 remains our model.

Who is the speaker? A person who has been rescued or saved almost always emerges as the one speaking in these psalms. Even when details are extremely sketchy, we sense the words of one who has genuinely experienced God's saving activity.

Who is being addressed? The psalmist addresses God numerous times (vv. 2, 3, 4, 8, 9, 10, 11, 12, 13), variously praising, thanking, calling for help, describing distress and saving actions. Once the psalmist calls on others, "you faithful" (v. 5). Presumably this indicates family, friends, and neighbors who have traveled to the shrine to join in this celebration of thanksgiving. They constitute the fellow worshipers at a shrine or the temple.

What is the mood? This psalm begins with a calm sense of gratitude, almost a note of quiet praise that God has healed and raised up this psalmist. After we have heard a description of the initial distress and outcry to God, the mood changes to exuberance: "You changed my mourning into dancing; you took off my sackcloth and clothed me with gladness" (v. 12). Dancing for joy portrays a crescendo of thanksgiving that resolves in a song with the entire being and endless praise. Most telling about the mood of the psalm is the alternation between sadness and joy and then the transformation of lamenting into rejoicing.

What does the psalmist desire? In these psalms the praying person's desires focus on other people: that all come to recognize God's goodness and saving love, that all join in this song of thanks to God for a wonderful rescue and concurrently sing praise to God for ways in which they too have been rescued. In verse 6 the psalmist clearly proclaims that any experience of God's anger is only temporary, that God's favor and our rejoicing will surely follow.

Finally, what images of God characterize this psalm? A helpful answer to this question begins by repeating all of the verbs that describe God's actions: "raised me up" (v. 2); "healed me" (v. 3); "brought me up from Sheol" (v. 4); "kept me from going down to the pit" (v. 4); "showed me favor" (v. 8); "hid your face" (v. 8); "changed my mourning into dancing" (v. 12); "took off my sackcloth" (v. 12); "clothed me with gladness" (v. 12). This psalmist describes a God of strong and specific actions, one personally engaged with the speaker, one who interacts by listening and responding. When we speak of thanksgiving psalms as prayers of a specific and concrete character, we also intend to express an experience of God as active and interactive, much more than a cosmic reality who orders and creates all things. These psalms offer an image of God personally and pointedly concerned for each person, a God who hears our cries and answers us, "who cares for the lowly," a God of enduring love and loyalty.

APPROPRIATING THANKSGIVING PSALMS FOR LIFE

The best hints about psalms of thanksgiving in our lives come from the psalm titles (superscriptions) that connect many psalms with the life and experiences of King David. Whether or not we feel certain that David wrote a certain psalm, these superscriptions connect specific events in David's life to psalms containing vocabulary and reasons for thanksgiving together with personal images of God. We frequently can return to a particular story in the Books of Samuel, read it, and imagine David praying in words very close to those in the psalm we are considering. The narrative about David activated the psalmist's imaginative powers toward vivid images and moods, so the psalm text itself may take on new life for hearers who can recall a similar experience and tap into a similar mood and set of emotions. John Calvin, for example, found great spiritual resources and comfort in pondering all the vicissitudes and sadness in the life of King David and comparing them to his own experience of leading the church in Geneva. When he prayed the psalms, his images of David allowed him to pray "as David did." He loved the psalms because he could also appropriate them for his life.

DAVID AND PSALMS OF THANKSGIVING

The Jewish community that inserted superscriptions to the psalms saw David as the premier example of one who prayed, sang, and composed these prayer songs. Contemplating his life and prayer, community members undoubtedly drew inspiration and strength for their own lives. Psalm 18's superscription clearly connects it with events in the life of David: "For the leader. Of David, the servant of the LORD, who sang to the LORD the words of this song after the LORD had rescued him from the clutches of all his enemies and from the hand of Saul" (RNAB). This psalm appears also in 2 Samuel 22; even the words of the superscription appear there in almost identical form. The writer in 2 Samuel incorporates the psalm into the flow of the narrative: "David spoke to the LORD the words of this song on the day when the LORD delivered him from the hand of all his enemies, and from the hand of Saul."

We might expect this psalm to appear earlier in the story of David; for example, after David escaped from Saul in the Judean desert (1 Sam 23:24–29). But its location near the end of the David story in Samuel is not too surprising, for the narrator in the Books of Samuel showed more interest in the theology and spirituality of 1—2 Samuel than in an exact chronology. He placed Hannah's song of thanksgiving at the beginning (1 Sam 2:1–10) and David's psalm of thanksgiving near the end (2 Sam 22:1–51). This story of David's rise, reign, and difficult court life begins and ends with songs of gratitude and thanksgiving.

As noted before, the superscription for Psalm 18 matches the words that introduce the psalm in 2 Samuel, suggesting that the composers of the Book of Psalms extracted it from this story. No wonder they connected many other psalms with events in David's life. If people could identify with aspects of David's life, the hopes, fears, joys, and sorrows of these psalms could reverberate within them.

Other thanksgiving psalms may recall David's life and spirituality. Psalm 30, which we examined in this chapter, has an unusually mixed superscription: "A psalm. A song for the dedication of the temple. Of David." Since David never dedicated a temple, this psalm may have originated as a "psalm of David" but reflected a wondrous transformation or healing in his life. In later centuries Jewish worshipers may have sung this psalm at a dedication ceremony for their temple, and so we witness a psalm of personal thanksgiving becoming a thanksgiving psalm of the community. True to the genre of thanksgiving, a personal event in the life of an individual has inspired and led many others to the same kind of celebration of thanks to God. Psalm 41 also thanks God for healing from sickness, and its superscription links it with David.

Several of these Davidic psalms render his thanks to God for preserving him from his enemies. Psalm 9 rejoices that enemies have been turned back (v. 4) and that God "rebuked the nations" (v. 6, RNAB); some commentators connect it with David's victories in 2 Samuel 8. Other psalms attributed to David and related to God saving him from his enemies are Psalm 34 ("of David; when he feigned madness before Abimelech, who forced him to depart."); Psalm 40:1–12, which many related to the time when Saul outlawed David (Cohen 1945, 123). Finally we mention Psalm 32, a penitential psalm whose superscription mentions David. Many commentators connect this psalm to David's sin with Bathsheba. Similarly, Psalm 51, known as the *Miserere* (from the Latin meaning "have mercy"), relates to these same events in David's life; David is sorrowing because of his affair with Bathsheba and his arranged murder of her husband, Uriah.

Three thanksgiving psalms that mention David in their superscriptions do not seem to connect with any particular events in his life or career. Psalm 65 articulates thanksgiving for a good harvest. Psalm 124 reflects gratitude for deliverance from recent danger. Psalm 138 is a lovely hymn of thanksgiving where the events seem very general; later it was also connected with Haggai and Zechariah in the Greek Septuagint version of the psalter. Perhaps these Davidic superscriptions demonstrate a general tendency to connect hymnody with David, traditional founder of the temple choirs staffed by the Levites.

All of these psalms can send us back to the Bible and its stories of David's vicissitudes, evoking feelings and thoughts appropriate to a story or a time in his life. In a parallel fashion, these psalms may call us to remember events in our own past or in the memory of our communities. Whenever this happens, we experience the power of the superscriptions to connect these psalms with concrete events in David's life or the lives of those who pray them.

HANNAH AND THANKSGIVING

In the description of laments we observed how Hannah had felt disgraced and worthless. She suffered a distress that could not be alleviated simply by kind words from her husband, even though he really loved her. The old priest Eli had given her hope: "Go in peace; the God of Israel grant the petition you have made to him" (1 Sam 1:17). Then her mood changed: She went back to her family quarters to dine with her husband and "her countenance was sad no longer" (1 Sam 1:18). When the entire family returned home to Ramah, she and her husband had sexual relations and "the LORD remembered her; in due time Hannah conceived and bore a son" (1 Sam 1:19b–20). Several years later Hannah went to the sanctuary to make her song and sacrifice of thanksgiving. The narrator supplies important details in 1 Samuel 1:24–28.

> When she had weaned him, she took him up with her, along with a three-year-old bull, an ephah of flour, and a skin of wine. She brought him to the house of the LORD at Shiloh; and the child was young. Then they slaughtered the bull, and they brought the child to Eli. And she said, "Oh, my Lord! As you live, my lord, I am the woman who was standing here in your

presence, praying to the LORD. For this child I prayed; and the LORD has granted me the petition that I made to him. Therefore I have lent him to the LORD; as long as he lives, he is given to the LORD.ʺ

Hannah's sacrifice at the shrine in Shiloh recalled her passionate prayer for a son, which had been graciously answered. When they slaughtered the bull, some meat went to the priests who tended the sanctuary, some was dedicated to God, and the rest was shared in a sacred meal with her extended family and intimates. This is what Elkanah did year by year, when he gave portions of the sacrifice to his wives.

Usually the narrator just hints at the prayer or song that is spoken or sung on such occasions, but here we have words, the famous Song of Hannah (1 Sam 2:1–10). Let us recall a few of its lines, which connect with her story of barrenness, prayer, promise, and birth of a child.

> 1 My heart exults in the LORD;
>   my strength is exalted in my God.
>   My mouth derides my enemies,
>   because I rejoice in my victory....
>
> 4 The bows of the mighty are broken,
>   but the feeble gird on strength....
> 5b The barren has borne seven,
>   but she who has many children is forlorn....
> 7 The LORD makes poor and makes rich;
>   he brings low, he also exalts.
> 8a He raises up the poor from the dust;
>   he lifts the needy from the ash heap,
>   to make them sit with princes
>   and inherit a seat of honor.

This exuberant song of thanksgiving refers to the birth of her child only by an allusion: the barren woman is contrasted with the mother of many (v. 5b). We can imagine Hannah identifying herself as one poor who has been made rich, one brought low and then made exultant. In its imagery this song thanks God for much more than Hannah's child's conception and birth: This song of exultation for gifts of restored life serves beautifully as a metaphor for Israel's own life as a people, raised up and saved from its enemies, guided by a king. Biblical scholars describe Hannah's prayer as a song of national thanksgiving, because this event in her life flowers into a joyful remembrance of God's continual, gracious response to Israel's ongoing need and lamentation.

In connecting her story with these words we can also connect our own stories of loss and new life with the words of this song of thanksgiving. Even more poignantly the words and images and motifs of this prayer song reappear in a prayer known even more widely, Mary's song of thanks after meeting with the angel Gabriel, the great *Magnificat* of prayer and tradition and musical settings (Luke 1:46–55). Hannah's song and Mary's song have helped generations of Christians to render thanks to God on a regular basis, especially when people sing or recite the *Magnificat* as part of the Liturgy of the Hours' Evening Prayer. There the *Magnificat* helps worshipers to reflect on their day with gratitude and praise. The time of day for this prayer carries a subtle spirituality, a movement from petition to gratitude as we live each day of our lives.

THANKSGIVING AND LAMENT

Hannah's passionate prayer for help reaches its completion in a joyful song of thanks to God. This pattern of lament and thanksgiving, as we saw in the chapter on laments, appeared within lament psalms themselves. We heard within one lament psalm a clear promise to give thanks to God: "I will sing to the Lord because he has

dealt bountifully with me" (Ps 13:6). In Psalm 22 we hear
the singer promise, "Then I will proclaim your name to
the assembly; in the community I will praise you" (v. 23).
Similar promises to make a public expression of gratitude
to God come elsewhere within lament psalms; we called
these vows of thanksgiving. These lines look forward to a
time of saving and rejoicing; they promise thanksgiving,
especially by singing God's goodness to the rest of the
congregation. They promise witness to the gracious activity of God.

Thanksgiving psalms put the focus on the vocal thanksgiving to God; they express the praise promised in the vow
of a lament. Psalms 9 and 10 are considered a single psalm
in the Greek and Latin versions, and they combine thanksgiving (Ps 9:1–13) and lament (Ps 9:14–21; Ps 10:1–18).
Psalm 9 begins with a song of exuberant thanksgiving (vv.
2–3) and then turns to the reasons for this public witness
(v. 4–5).

> 2   I will praise you, LORD, with all my heart;
>   I will declare all your wondrous deeds.
> 3   I will delight and rejoice in you;
>   I will sing hymns to your name, Most High.
> 4   For my enemies turn back;
>   they stumble and perish before you.
> 5   You upheld my right and my cause,
>   seated on your throne, judging justly. (RNAB)

The psalmist further builds up the defeat of the enemies in
verses 6–7. This psalm proclaims that God acted when
distress was alleviated. Just as the lament points to particular situations of distress, so also thanksgiving psalms
refer to specific situations of divine intervention. In other
words, the relation between lament and thanksgiving may
be described as that between anticipation and response to
God's action. In psalms, genuine thanksgiving relates to

laments, when urgent crying to God in need is transformed into thanksgiving for God's actions.

In thanksgiving psalms the vow to thank God has become a reality, and the psalmist describes the need that required God's help. Whenever we pray with thanksgiving psalms we can remember that they are grounded in concrete, not generic, situations. Proclaimed in the midst of a worshiping assembly, thanksgiving is concrete and personal but not private, for it is shared with all.

THANKSGIVING AND SACRIFICE

Thanksgiving often takes the form of sacrifice as well as song and prayer. Again the thanksgiving psalm corresponds to the lament: Often the lamenter vowed to God to offer sacrifices if God intervened. An excellent example emerges at the end of Psalm 56 (lament).

> 13 I have made vows to you, God:
>   with offerings I will fulfill them,
> 14 Once you have snatched me from death,
>   kept my feet from stumbling,
>   That I may walk before God
>   in the light of the living. (RNAB)

When God saves the life of this lamenter, he or she will fulfill this vow with thank-offerings.

This pattern of prayer for help coupled with a vow to offer sacrifice continues in Hannah's story, and it remains instructive. She expressed thanksgiving to the God who answered her prayer both with words and a sacrificial meal. She took to the sanctuary at Shiloh "a three-year-old bull, an ephah of flour, and a skin of wine." Often in Israel the expression of gratitude to God came not only in prayer but also in food offerings made at the sanctuary. In Leviticus 7:11–15 the writer describes "sacrifices of thanksgiving" that people bring to the altar, using a Hebrew word, *todah*. We can translate todah as "sacrifice of thanksgiving," but it also signifies a religious sense of thanksgiving (Levine 1995, 42) and a proclamation of thanksgiving.

So the Hebrew word for thanksgiving covers the feeling of gratitude and also the proclamation of it in song or prayer and sacrifice of thanksgiving offered to God. Usually the thanksgiving ceremony included all three elements, and the food offered in sacrifice was shared with all the people who accompanied the grateful person to the shrine of God as well as with the priests who cared for the shrine. It is possible to consider this a kind of communion meal, a meal shared with other believers *(communio)* that proclaims thanksgiving to God. The story of Hannah reminds us not only of her desperation and cry to God, but also of her thanksgiving sacrifice and the meal with which she celebrated her gratitude. Within psalms of thanksgiving and stories of thanksgiving like Hannah's, we find the depths of gratitude to God expressed both in prayer song and in shared sacrifices and meals.

THANKSGIVING PSALMS AND EUCHARIST

Grateful acknowledgment of God's concrete gifts to us forms the basis of the Christian celebration of the Lord's Supper, which many of us call the Eucharist. The Greek root word *eucharisteo* means "to give thanks," and it characterizes worship with this significance. The basic format of Eucharist is giving thanks to God in the company of worshipers: for the gifts of creation; for the life, death, and resurrection of Jesus; for the new life God gives us. Like Elkanah and Hannah, we bring sacrificial gifts and then share a communion meal together, worshiping God as we partake of a sacred meal. In Christian history two psalms have been frequently described as eucharistic psalms:

Psalms 34 and 66 (especially vv. 13–20). These psalms provide wonderful food for prayer, just as they have so often accompanied the celebration of the "bread come down from heaven," the "bread of life." Psalm 34, in particular, has been a favorite text for musical settings, especially those connected with Eucharist. Finally, Psalm 116 also has strong connections with gratitude and the Christian Eucharist, and many Christian churches assign this psalm to the liturgies for Thursday of Holy Week, when worshipers commemorate Christ's institution of the Eucharist.

To summarize: Thanksgiving psalms teach us a way to express gratitude to God for responding to our concrete needs and urgent petitions (usually uttered in laments). They often grace rituals that proclaim the goodness of God, both in the life of Israel and in our day. As we ponder and pray these songs of thanksgiving, may we grow to recognize more deeply all of God's gifts to us and to proclaim and celebrate our gratitude with all people.

PRAYING THANKSGIVING PSALMS

Thanksgiving follows lament as God hears our cry. Some thanksgiving psalms that stress individual thanksgiving are Psalms 9, 18, 30, 32, 34, 40, 92, 116, and 138. Some thanksgiving psalms are embedded in other books of the Bible, such as Isaiah 38:9–20, Jonah 2:2–9. Psalms that express the community's thanksgiving include Psalms 65, 66, 67, 75, 107, and 124. A number of psalms focus so much energy on trust or confidence in God that they are often called psalms of trust. They include Psalms 16, 23, 27, 63, 91, 115, 121, and 131. (For complete lists please consult Appendix 1, "Psalms by Type.")

ALLOWING THANKSGIVING TO ARISE

Since gratitude and thanksgiving arise within us as we become aware of others' graciousness toward us, we can nurture a thankful heart by cultivating attention to God's constant and lavish gifts. The following mindfulness exercises can be practiced in long or short time spans. They require no text other than what is already happening to us. They invite us to turn aside from a habit of doing multiple tasks at the same moment, a habit that can be hard to break.

1. Eating a meal. Washing the dishes. Folding the laundry. Mowing the lawn. Washing the car. Pulling weeds. Dusting. Washing your hands. Pick one of these tasks or another of your choice and do it with complete attention. When you notice your mind wandering, gently bring it back to your chosen task. *When you are eating, eat,* as the saying goes. Consciously do what you are doing in God's presence. Notice your feelings as you practice mindfulness of your chosen task.

2. If you are able, take a slow walk for a short distance: around the block, up and down the corridors of an office building, around a school yard, through your neighborhood. You are not going anywhere; you have no destination. You are simply walking contemplatively, noticing and savoring. If you cannot walk unaided, invite someone to join you in this exercise.

First, notice your surroundings. What is there? What light, color, sound, smell, texture? Take it all in. Savor it. Pause when something draws you. Notice it deeply but without judging its usefulness, beauty, appropriateness. Simply allow it to be whatever it is. Honor it in its otherness. Now notice yourself walking. What does walking feel like? What sensations occur in your muscles, bones, skin? Notice how your body balances itself, usually without any conscious intervention on your part. Does your body feel ready to do more? Less? Honor it.

3. Relive in your memory an experience for which you are particularly grateful, perhaps the birth of a child, an illness overcome or eased, employment received, a friendship formed. See all the players, experience the event again. Recall what you did, what was done to or for you. Name all the elements that make up this gift to you. Express to God in your own words the gratitude you feel.

4. Notice a situation in which a service person is virtually invisible, possibly the bagger at the grocery store, the janitor in your office or apartment, the faceless person who takes your order over the telephone. Express thanks, not only for the service, but for his or her very person. Your thanks may not look or sound any different outwardly, but inwardly you can have heightened mindfulness of the unique person before you.

5. When someone compliments you, simply say "thank you" without making any excuses or qualifications or turning the compliment aside in any way. Compliment others when you see a gift or quality in them.

6. In your mind's eye gaze on a particular person with love. Be present to this person, a loved one, a stranger, a child, a parent, a friend, or an enemy. Let the person be in your heart, held there gently and lovingly, nonpossessively.

WRITING YOUR OWN PSALM OF THANKSGIVING

• Using the form suggested in this chapter (introduction, reason for thanking God, calling others to thank God, and giving thanks and praise to God) write your own psalm of thanksgiving. Psalm 40:1–10 can serve as a model.

HANDMADE MIDRASH

• Using the thanksgiving psalm you wrote yourself or selecting another thanksgiving psalm, ponder it until you become aware of the "center" of your thanksgiving. If you are working with a biblical psalm, you may find it helpful to consult a commentary.

• Now select materials for your handmade midrash. They can be any materials available to you: cloth, paper, crayons, pencils, ink, glue, sticks, grasses or dried flowers, buttons, seeds, rice or wheat, photographs, pictures from magazines. Arrange them so that they express your sense of thankfulness.

• Discuss your creation with another person. Use the suggestions in chapter 2 to guide this conversation.

• Write in your journal, using some or all of the suggestions in chapter 2.

• Reflect: How does the psalm now speak to or for you?

PRAYING THE *MAGNIFICAT*

• For centuries, Hannah's song (1 Sam 2:1–10) and Mary's song (Luke 1:46–55) have guided personal and corporate thanksgiving prayer. Pray Mary's canticle slowly, imaginatively, repetitively. Ask these questions of the text: Who is the speaker? Whom does she address? What is the mood? What does she desire? Who is the God addressed in this prayer? Select a verse and stay with it in the manner of *lectio divina*. Perhaps you will want to express Mary's song of thanksgiving with a handmade midrash. Sing it, if you have a setting available. Allow the cadence and images of the prayer to seep into your spirit.

SINGING THE THANKSGIVING PSALMS

• From the list of hymns below, select a thanksgiving psalm known to you and sing it several times, until it has impressed itself upon you. Try to memorize a portion of the psalm in this musical setting and sing it (interiorly or aloud) throughout the day. On another day select another thanksgiving psalm setting and repeat the process. The last three hymns, though not related to specific psalms, capture the mood and substance of Christian thanksgiving.

Psalm	Title	Tune/Composer	Hymnal
9	Amen. Siakudumisa	Molefe (Iona)	G
18	Thee Will I Love, My Strength	Ich Will Dich Lieben	LBW
30	I Will Praise You	Inwood	G, G&P
32	How Blest Are Those	Es Flog Ein Kleins…	PH
34	The Cry of the Poor	Foley	G, G&P
66	Glory and Praise to Our God	Schutte	G, G&P
116	O Thou My Soul, Return in Peace	Smallwood, CM	PH, NCH
116	Our Blessing Cup	Joncas	G&P
124	Now Israel May Sing	Old 124th	PH
138	Great Is the Glory	Diemer	NCH, P
general	For the Beauty	Lucerna Laudoniae	PH, W, G
	Now Thank We All Our God	Nun Danket alle Gott	PH, W, G
	Let All Things Now Living	Ash Grove	PH, W, G

CORPORATE PSALM PRAYER:
EVENING PRAYEROF THANKSGIVING

• Pray, with a group if possible, the following Evening
Prayer. Use your community's hymnal to select appropriate psalms, hymns, and antiphons for singing. The psalm
prayers, thanksgiving, and dismissal in the following service are adapted from *Daily Prayer* 1987, 239 alt, 279, 86.

Service of Light
   Greeting: Light and peace in Jesus Christ our Lord.
   Thanks be to God.
   Hymn: "Phos Hilaron" or another suitable evening
   hymn

Psalm 34 (sung or recited antiphonally)

Psalm Prayer
   God, most bounteous, help us to receive all as gift
   and give you thanks that you are our God. Continue
   to grant us your joy and your peace and help us to
   share your gifts with all in need. This we ask through
   Jesus, who lives with you and the Holy Spirit forever
   and ever. **Amen.**

Psalm 116 (sung or recited antiphonally)

Psalm Prayer
   God, you came to set us free in Jesus Christ. Give us
   hope in him that our lives may be renewed and that
   we may fulfill our vows to Christ, as you have kept
   all promises in him. **Amen.**

Reading: Luke 17:11–19

Silent reflection (or brief homily)

Gospel Canticle: Canticle of Mary (sung or recited
antiphonally)

Prayers of Thanksgiving
> Let us rejoice in our God who takes great delight in bestowing benefits on all people. Let us pray:
> For the beauty of your creation, **we give you thanks.**
> For gifts of healing and forgiveness, **we give you thanks.**
> For the sustaining love of family and friends,
> **we give you thanks.**
> For the community of believers in your church,
> **we give you thanks.**
> For whom or for what else shall we give thanks?
> (participants mention reasons for thanks),
> **we give you thanks.**

The Lord's Prayer

Concluding Prayer
> Gracious God, holy is your name and renowned your compassion, cherished by every generation. Hear our evening prayer and let us sing your praise and proclaim your greatness forever. We ask this in the name of Jesus Christ our brother and friend. **Amen.**
> To God be honor and glory forever! (1 Tim 1:17) **Amen.**
> Bless the Lord. **The Lord's name be praised.**

Psalm 29

1   A psalm of David.

    I

2   Give to the LORD, you heavenly beings,
    give to the LORD glory and might;
    Give to the LORD the glory due God's name.
    Bow down before the LORD's holy splendor!

    II

3   The voice of the LORD is over the waters;
    the God of glory thunders,
    the LORD, over the mighty waters.
4   The voice of the LORD is power;
    the voice of the LORD is splendor.
5   The voice of the LORD cracks the cedars;
    the LORD splinters the cedars of Lebanon,
6   Makes Lebanon leap like a calf,
    and Sirion like a young bull.
7   The voice of the LORD strikes with fiery flame;
8   the voice of the LORD rocks the desert;
    the LORD rocks the desert of Kadesh.
9   The voice of the LORD twists the oaks
    and strips the forests bare.
    All in his palace say, "Glory!"

    III

10 The LORD sits enthroned above the flood!
    The LORD reigns as king forever!
11 May the LORD give might to his people;
    may the LORD bless his people with peace!
    (RNAB)

Six
Singing to God in Worship: Psalms of Praise

In everyday life most people easily distinguish between the actions of praising and thanking others. To thank someone for a wonderful deed or gift marks a person as grateful, but such expressions do not move far beyond normal expectations. Praising someone, however, involves descriptive phrases that build on one another to paint an overall picture of greatness or beauty or wisdom. Verbal praise has the power to trigger both surprise and delight, especially when the praise comes for no particular reason. Consider the child whose grandfather lovingly proclaims all her good qualities to the entire family or the engaged couple whose conversation often includes a litany of reasons "why I love you." It's not difficult to imagine why they bask in the praise they receive. A major difference between praise and thanksgiving, then, is the gratuitous nature of praise. Another important difference has to do with the scope of praise. Gratitude usually focuses on a specific instance, while praise generally paints a portrait of diverse and beautiful features. Both types of expression are important, but they express different feelings and discourse.

What does it mean to praise God? Whenever we look at the exquisite beauty of the world around us—the beauty of the mountains or the sea, sunrise or sunset, beautiful flora or fauna, the stars and moon at night—and spontaneously wish to acclaim God for it all, then we are praising God. When we become aware of the ways people have been freed to live together as they wish, to work and express themselves freely, to worship as they want, then we can praise God, whom we find involved in all of this liberating movement. If we are part of a worshiping group that genuinely experiences God's movement, then we know the desire to praise. Whenever we truly pray or sing the Doxology—"Glory be to the Father, and to the Son, and to the Holy Spirit"—we experience praise. Many hymns that we pray or sing primarily give praise to God.

Still, many people wonder if it isn't enough to call on God in our need and to thank God when we experience a reversal for the good. In other words, does praise differ in any important way from expressing our gratitude to God? After all, we often transfer direct feelings and expressions of gratitude into the realm of thanks and praise to God. Confusion between praise and thanksgiving in worship and song is not infrequent. Some psalms of thanksgiving actually use the language of praise in their address to God, so the confusion between the two types may come from the psalms themselves.

Many people today gravitate toward more personal religious expression than their traditions seem to espouse. This trend often focuses on Jesus as friend or brother and prefers the language of human relationships. Such prayer regularly emerges in smaller Christian communities or groups where the bonds among members are particularly strong and important. And many Roman Catholics developed this emphasis in post–Vatican II spirituality, made possible by the celebration of public worship in vernacular languages. But the liturgical changes did not satisfy the desires of all Catholic worshipers. Many continued to pray the Rosary and other private devotions during the Mass, even though it was now celebrated in the vernacular. Perhaps this ambivalence between full participation and presence at Mass represents a continuing desire for a more personal type of prayer or spirituality.

The personal vs. group nature of prayer points to another very important aspect of praying with psalms of praise: These psalms usually derive from a communal setting. They correspond to festive song and dance, chanting or singing all God's praises in some kind of unity. Certain kinds of music lend themselves particularly well to praise; the psalms of praise seem best suited to music played on a pipe organ, which can fill a large space with sound. When we hear such hymns of praise, we have a sense of the majestic space of churches with long, high naves, likely to be cathedrals or Gothic churches. Such structures themselves evoke a sense of the eternal heavenly heights.

Some contemporary religious and cultural notions make a sense of praise difficult to sustain. An immediate and personalist view of our spiritual lives may correspond to a horizontal view of our cosmos. Concern with the here and now, interactions with others, and images of our relationship with Jesus as personal contrast with notions like eternal truths, unchanging law, heavenly realities—all these aspects of personal and communal worldviews can contribute to a sense that this world is what really counts. Notions of another realm in space or time feel odd or antiquated to some people. Concern for this world rather than the heavenly realm also dramatizes a distinction in feeling between horizontal and vertical relationships.

Hymns of praise frequently play on a notion of vertical space, which brings comfort to some people but a sense of awkwardness or alienation to others. When we develop more vertical sensibilities, however, we reach out further in space and time. The words and music of hymns tend to move outward, to the heavens above as well as to the very ends of the earth. A quality of timelessness allows them to speak to the distant past and to the future. We can expect to discover a more expansive cosmology and sense of all creation in these psalms. We can also imagine a longer history of God's saving and liberating activity among God's people throughout generations. Praise psalms open us to the expanse of space and time, just as thanksgiving psalms focus on the personal and particular aspects of our experience. A healthy tension between a this-worldly and an otherworldly vision of existence creates a more balanced spirituality. This class of psalms may help to redress some recent imbalances.

PRAISE PSALMS AS A TYPE

In the chapter on laments we spoke of psalms that have the power to touch us very deeply, to penetrate the depths of our feelings and psyches, individual and communal. Now we explore psalms that often move us in the opposite direction—psalms that lift us up, that carry us along, that remind us of the timelessness and the grandeur of God's creation and space. They seldom project the voice of one individual, so suited are they to the song of jubilation and exuberance that only finds its home in larger communities or congregations. Although specialists often call these psalms hymns, we prefer to speak of them as praise psalms to avoid confusion with the generic word *hymn* as used in church context. No matter what they are called, these are psalms sung in large groups that raise joyful noise to God, taking the worshiper along. Such psalms celebrate the immensity of God's goodness and love through all the ages of our existence or throughout the inhabited world. They remind us of the great breadth and abundance of the world God created, from the heavens above to the earth below. Psalm 148 is a fine example, calling for praise to God from the heavens (v. 1) and from the earth (v. 7).

Israel praised God for many reasons, especially because God brought them out of Egypt and saved them from the house of bondage. The shortest praise song, found in Exodus rather than in the Book of Psalms, speaks of the jubilation of the Hebrews. In Exodus 15:20–21 we read:

> Then the prophet Miriam, Aaron's sister, took a tambourine in her hand; and all the women went out after her with tambourines and with dancing. And Miriam sang to them: "Sing to the LORD, for he has triumphed gloriously; horse and rider he has thrown into the sea."

Miriam's song contains the essential elements of a psalm of praise. She tells her community what to do in order to praise God: "sing to the LORD." Then she proclaims the reason for such praise: "for he has triumphed gloriously; horse and rider he has thrown into the sea." The Song of Moses, which precedes this praise psalm, presents an expanded version of this hymn.

STRUCTURE OF PSALMS OF PRAISE

In the shortest of the psalms, Psalm 117, we see all the elements of a praise psalm. Someone gives an order to praise the LORD, and it is addressed to all nations. In quick succession the leader repeats the call to worship. There follows the reason for praise.

> 1 *Praise* the LORD, all you nations!
>   *Give glory,* all you peoples!
> 2 The LORD's love for us is strong;
>   the LORD is faithful forever.
>   *Hallelujah!* (RNAB)

Call to Praise/Worship: "Praise the LORD" and "Give glory" (v. 1). Often the call to praise is contained in a verb found in the imperative, giving a command to someone or some group. In some cases the leader begins in the first person; for example

> I will extol you, my God and king;
>   I will bless your name forever. (Ps 145:1, RNAB)

An interesting variation on the imperative verb with first person is the following: "Praise the LORD, my soul; I shall praise the LORD all my life" (Ps 146:1b–2a, RNAB). In Psalm 117 the reason for praising God comes in verse 2, which extols God's love and fidelity. Many praise psalms introduce the reasons for praise with a word like *for* or *because* (omitted in the translation of this psalm), which frequently points to the main section of the hymn, a listing of all God's actions and attributes. Here it consists of God's continuing ways of relating to Israel: God's love and fidelity toward "us." The words *love* and *fidelity* often appear together in the Hebrew scriptures, especially in the psalms; they convey a rich sense of the covenantal bond of love with the people chosen and created by God. This psalm calls on all the surrounding peoples and nations to praise God for the aspects of God's relationship with the people chosen by and in this covenantal relationship. The call to worship expands our vision of those who worship God, while the reason for praise zeroes in on Israel. Does the psalmist hint that Israel's life with God is so extraordinary that other nations and peoples should praise their God? This psalm and several others clearly point in that direction.

Usually praise psalms begin with this call to praise or worship. We may imagine that someone has taken the initiative, telling some group to praise God. The verbs are imperatives or exhortations: "give glory and praise," "rejoice," "clap your hands," "shout joyfully," "sing," "sing a new song," "worship," "praise," "bless," "lift up your hands," "extol." By paying careful attention to the openings verses we can learn much about the worship of God envisioned in these psalms of praise. For example, the identity of worshipers emerges from listening to who is called to praise God: "you just," "you heavenly beings," "you peoples," "all on earth," "the earth," "all you lands," "peoples," "nations," "heavenly beings," "angels," "all creatures of the heavens or the earth," "servants of the LORD," "Jerusalem," "angels," "sun and moon," "shining stars," "heavens," "sea monsters and deep waters," "lightning," "hail," "snow," "clouds," "animals," "creatures that crawl and fly," "kings of the earth," "young men," "women," "old and young," "Israel," "people of Zion," "everything that has breath." Of course, God's faithful people receive the invitation to praise most often, but all peoples are expected to join it. The list above shows how cosmic is the notion of praise and worship of God; it even includes animals, heavenly bodies, and indeed everything that breathes. Everything created by God should join in jubilant praise of God. The range is far more cosmic than personal.

Reasons for Praise: The reasons to praise God cover almost every aspect of our existence—God's history of saving this people, especially God's saving activity in the past (e.g., Exod 15:21; Pss 111, 114, and 135—36), or the expanse of God's creative and sustaining activity in the world (e.g., Pss 8, 19, 29, 33, 103, and 104). Some psalms praise God's "loving kindness and fidelity," especially to covenant members who have suffered poverty and oppression (Pss 113, 145, and 146). Thus the motives for praise come both from the past (God's actions in history) and from the present (God's continual loving activity). The Hebrew text of the psalms carefully distinguishes the past (with a perfect tense, which signifies past action) from continuing, present activity (with a present participle, like "covering, bending down, raising up"); the latter seem especially difficult to render into English. A good example appears in the early verses of Psalm 103; English words that translate Hebrew participles appear in italics.

> 2 Bless the LORD, my soul;
>   do not forget all the gifts of God,
> 3 *Who pardons* all your sins,
>   *heals* all your ills. (RNAB)

A literal rendering of verse 3 might be: "who *is pardoning* all your sins, *healing* all your ills." The -*ing* ending suggests a form that is less restrictive with regard to time; it may point to both present and future and sometimes even the past. The participial verb form signifies enduring and even timeless qualities rather than specific actions in space and time. The grammar of these psalms matches the type of the psalm, the hymn of praise with its description of God.

Many people in biblical times experienced such saving activity by God, but the psalmist is not satisfied with the past. God continues pardoning, healing, delivering, surrounding us with love and compassion (Ps 103:4–5). In other hymns where the wonders of creation provide a reason to praise God, the continuing creative activity of God impresses itself on us through use of participles. God created and creates, began and continues creation; God's creativity did not cease to occur after a particular time. When theologians speak of *creatio continua* (creation continuing), they certainly express the joy of the hymns of praise.

Final Call to Praise God: This psalm ends with a concluding call to praise God by shouting out, "Hallelujah!" This English word, often rendered Alleluia, comes directly from the Hebrew. *Hallelu* in Hebrew means "shout, sing praise"; *-yah* is an abbreviation for Yahweh (YHWH), the special and personal name of God that observant Jews do not pronounce and that is translated as LORD in most English translations of the Bible. So this psalm ends by repeating the brief call to praise or worship. There are several other psalms that conclude with a Hallelujah, such as Psalms 104, 105, 106, 115, 117, 135, 146, 147, 148, 149, and 150. It also occurs at the beginning of Psalms 106, 111, 112, 113, 135, 146, 147, 148, 149, and 150. This heading is not conclusive evidence of a praise psalm—many of them lack it—but when it appears it usually indicates this type of psalm.

QUESTIONS WHEN READING PRAISE PSALMS

Earlier we spoke of Miriam's song as the simplest example of a song or psalm of praise. Even with such a brief song (Exod 15:21) we can pose the same questions that have helped us to describe the other kinds of psalms we have been pondering.

• Who is speaking? In this song it is Miriam, Aaron's sister—she leads part of the worship.

• Who should sing? Everyone who observed the events at the sea should sing out praise. All of us who hear the story now should also sing praise, for the crossing of the sea is an important part of our faith history. Many Christians incorporate this song into their celebration of the victory of Christ's resurrection at the Easter Vigil.
• What is the mood? It is one of jubilant praise—how happy we are after generations of servitude and suffering!

APPROPRIATING PRAISE PSALMS FOR LIFE

In laments and thanksgiving psalms the core of the action and the focus of attention is usually found in the vicissitudes and joys of everyday life. Praise psalms, on the other hand, have a distinctive worldview: They stretch from the ends of the earth to the highest heavens above earth. These psalms speak of the heavens and the earth more than any other type of psalm, and this language draws us beyond the boundaries of normal human experience. As we contemplate the cosmos behind Psalm 29, we find ourselves in a universe that is often described as two-tiered: the heavens and the earth. This psalm reminds us that we humans on earth are not alone: There is a world above that also praises God.

1   Give to the LORD, *you heavenly beings,*
       give to the LORD glory and might;
2   Give to the LORD the glory due God's name.
       Bow down before the LORD's holy splendor.
    (RNAB)

Sometimes our translations make these heavenly beings "angels," at other times minor "gods." Amazingly, people on earth, in the temple, are calling on heavenly beings to worship the LORD, just as we do. Someone in the temple is speaking. Those who live in the heavens are listening (as are those on earth, especially in the temple). They are not only to sing praise and shout "glory," they are also to bow down before God's splendor. They should worship in song and gesture. We moderns—especially in the Western world—could easily ignore this aspect of the psalm by considering it just another anthropomorphism, viewing God or other heavenly beings through typical human characteristics. This heavenly call to worship, however, draws us into an important aspect of psalmic spirituality, the cosmic sphere.

In Psalm 29 the "voice of the LORD" moves powerfully across the earth, in thunder and power, in lightning, probably in heavy rains and destructive winds (29:3–9). The power of God is manifest in raging storms, an idea that remains with many people today. But an important point in this psalm is the LORD's "residence" in the final verses of the psalm:

9c   All in his palace say, "Glory!"
10   The LORD sits enthroned above the flood!
      The LORD reigns as king forever!
11   May the LORD give might to his people;
      may the LORD bless his people with peace!

In Hebrew cosmology "above the flood" is the upper flood, the clouds above the skies where the rainwaters are held back from drowning the earth. That is where God's palace is, and everyone in this palace shouts "glory" or some liturgical song with a similar opening (such as the refrain in the "Battle Hymn of the Republic," which begins, "Glory, glory, Halleluia!"). The powerful voice of the LORD has reverberated from the heavenly court, wreaked destruction and also brought the drenching rains that lead to fertility on the earth—a vision of God acting in a fashion so crucial to the agrarian and pastoral societies of the Middle East. But it all begins in the heavens, and there it ends with songs of praise to God.

The worldview here corresponds to that in the first chapter of Genesis. The earth on which we stand is poised on huge pillars that protect us from the lower waters; over the earth is a firmament, covering us like a bowl, which corresponds to our view of the clouds in the heavens. God's palace, the heavenly temple, stands above the firmament, and at the divine throne God meets angels and other heavenly beings. Rain floods down when the windows of the firmament are opened. God's house in the heavens serves also as a place of praise and worship, especially when the heavenly beings that reside there are singing songs of praise and worship.

This cosmic picture describes a common religious view in the Ancient Near East, but in Israel it takes on special characteristics. In biblical religion the heavenly court has only one supreme God, while all the others—called gods in other religions—are some kind of heavenly beings in Israel, which they later described as angels of God. In the Ancient Near East all activity in the temple on earth is understood to correspond to that in the god's house or palace in heaven, so the earthly palace simply mirrors or reflects the heavenly reality as well as possible. The religion of the Jerusalem Temple shares in this worldview, especially with the praise psalms that focus so often on heavenly beings summoned to worship at the same time as the prayer and worship in the earthly Temple. In a real sense the psalm leader in Jerusalem calls on the heavenly courts to begin singing and worshiping God in the heavenly temple; then both worship services can proceed in harmony.

Recent terminology capturing this notion is that of the "heavenly liturgy," a rather arcane concept unless we imagine a two-tiered universe. This cosmic view is problematic for those who view the world as limited to that which we can perceive with our senses. But there is another worldview that can enrich our imaginative and interior lives; it is often illustrated in the architectural design and construction of Eastern or Byzantine churches, which often are laid out in cruciform design, the pillars of the crossing supporting a huge dome filled with icons. The icon-covered dome reflects the heavenly reality, with a Christ Pantokrator (ruler over all) at its center. A standard order fills out the design: First, there is a row of angels, many of them with musical instruments, some with incense, all clearly engaged in a heavenly liturgy. At lower levels there are icons of famous patriarchs of the church, other saints, apostles, and finally the four evangelists. All of these spread out from the Christic center of the dome, and if one contemplates the entire scene, a liturgy of the entire heavenly court begins to emerge. For those standing on the floor below during the liturgy, there is a sense that their prayer participates in the heavenly liturgy. One might even imagine that the liturgical activity in the church corresponds to and invites those in the heavens to begin their praise and song. To pray in this fashion is to share in a two-tiered universe, at least in the aesthetic and imaginative realms: The worshiping congregation is part of the heavenly liturgy of praise.

REASONS FOR PRAISING GOD

In psalms of praise one needs to ask, What are they praising? In Psalm 29 the heavenly beings praise "the voice of the LORD," experienced metaphorically in thunderstorms, lightning, power in the heavens, and the bringing of rain to the parched earth. When we pray this psalm we praise the ruler of the heavens, the LORD of the storm, the God who brings life and fertility to the land with the rains brought by storms wrought by God's thundering voice. Some praise psalms extol other aspects and manifestations of God's creating activity, and they may even invite all creation, every created being in the heavens and on the earth, everything "that has breath" to join in the praise. Or they may focus on God's abiding love and guidance for Israel, stretching from God's constitutive act of bringing this people out of Egypt to its continuing life and role as worshiping community. Such psalms have an air of tradition, of a happy history of God's actions rather than the flavor of a recent intervention by God. The mood that prevails is usually one of jubilance, happiness, delight, and praise. We praise God because God loves the entire created world with a mighty love that never dies out, that is ever faithful.

In Israel these psalms were hymns of the Jerusalem Temple, so they may have been chanted and sung at daily worship, when morning and evening sacrifices were offered, by choirs of Levites in festival processions. This practice seems more characteristic of the life of the Temple after the exile in Babylon, and many of our examples of psalms chanted in the Temple come from the Books of Chronicles. These are songs of a community; they are songs of splendor. Israel's praise psalms can be sung outside of the Temple, of course, but they feel different in a new landscape.

To summarize: Psalms of praise invite us into a cosmic worldview that is truly "long distance"—it draws on Ancient Near Eastern perceptions of the universe and offers glimpses of worship in the Jerusalem Temple. These psalms accentuate the vertical relationship with God, the creator and ruler of the universe, a two-tiered worldview in which our life on earth both mirrors and is mirrored by the heavenly realms. These psalms may seem more at home in a Byzantine church than in Western church structures, but they offer us beautiful opportunities to fix our gaze on the heavens above and the earth to its very limits, all creations of the God we worship with these psalms. If the music of a hymn of praise overwhelms us, it serves us well, reminding us that we exist and live in a universe far greater than our own limited space and time. But praise psalms do not call us to consider ourselves insignificant; on the contrary, we can call all the universe, even the angels and heavenly beings, to worship in song and praise! Hallelujah!

PRAYING PRAISE PSALMS

A great collection of praise psalms occurs at the end of the psalter, Psalms 145—150, traditionally used for Morning Prayer. Other praise psalms include Psalms 29, 95, 103, 104, and 117. Psalm 95 has served as a daily call to worship in both Jewish and Christian traditions for centuries. A number of psalms praise God because of the divine choice of Jerusalem as site of the Temple and monarchy; these are often called Songs of Zion. (For more complete lists of praise psalms, please consult Appendix 1, "Psalms by Type.")

PRAISE FOR ALL THAT LIFE BRINGS

Psalm 145 praises God for both good and bad things—nothing is omitted. Those who recite it three times a day in the synagogue are assured of inheriting the world to come—after all, who can be lost who praises God for all things, morning, noon, and night?
• Look back over your week. Praise God for the happy moments that were special to you. Praise God for the moments that were difficult, too (Fritz 1995, 16–17).

IN PRAISE OF CREATION

• Many praise psalms extol creation and the creator, for example, Psalms 29, 104, and 148. Go for a walk, if possible in a place where nature is unspoiled. If such a place is not available, seek nature wherever you find it, even in the middle of the city. Attend to what you find, either on a large scale (a mountain vista or ocean breakers) or small (a single flower or insect), as you are led. Pray repeatedly: "Bless the LORD, my soul! LORD, my God, you are great indeed!" (Ps 104:1).

EXPRESSING PRAISE PSALMS IN MOVEMENT

Shuking: Try adding a simple movement called *shuking* to your prayer of praise. Lift up your hands in praise or fold your arms across your heart in an embrace and sway from side to side or back and forth in time with your singing: Put your whole body into the song (Fritz 1995, 78).

Victory Dance! This movement prayer lends itself to a group. Together read Exodus 15, a praise psalm of victory over the Egyptians. Spend some time probing its meaning, both then and now. Using some of the suggestions in chapter 2, create together a danced expression of 15:20–21. While some dance, other participants may join by playing musical "instruments": spoons, glasses, pans, empty oatmeal boxes, blocks, and the like. Or visit your local school's music department and borrow a supply of percussion instruments. Share your dance in an appropriate setting.

WRITING YOUR OWN PRAISE PSALM

• Write your own prayer. You might want to use the format of these verses from Psalm 103:20–21:

Bless the LORD...
Bless the LORD...
Bless the LORD...
Bless the LORD, O my soul.

• Or simply write your own praise psalm in any form you choose. Before you begin, you might wish to read Psalm 146 (an individual), Psalm 147 (the people), and Psalm 148 (creation).

SINGING THE PRAISE PSALMS

• Select a praise psalm known to you, perhaps one listed in your tradition's hymnal, and sing it until the hymn has impressed itself upon you. Try to memorize a portion of the psalm in this musical setting and sing it (interiorly or aloud) throughout the day. On another day select another setting and repeat the process.

Psalm	Title	Tune/Composer	Hymnal
19	Cantemos Al Señor	Rosas	UMH, G, WOV
24	Lift Up Your Heads, Ye Mighty Gates	Truro LM	PH, UMH, NCH, W
24	All Glory, Laud, and Honor	St. Theodulph	most hymnals
33	There's a Wideness in God's Mercy	In Babilone	PH, W, G, G&P
98	Joy to the World	Antioch	most hymnals

100	All People That on Earth Do Dwell	Old Hundredth	most hymnals
103	Praise My Soul the King of Heaven	Lauda Anima	most hymnals
104	Praise to the Lord	Lobe Den Herren	most hymnals
104	Joyful, Joyful, We Adore Thee	Hymn to Joy	most hymnals
104	O That I Had a Thous and Voices	O Das Ich Tausend Zungen Hätte	PH, W, LBW
117	From All That Dwell Below the Skies	Duke Street LM	UMH, W, HEC
148	All Creatures of Our God and King (To You O God ...)	Lasst Uns Erfreuen	most hymnals
148	For the Beauty of the Earth	Dix	most hymnals

CORPORATE PSALM PRAYER: MORNING PRAYER OF PRAISE

• Pray, with a group if possible, the following Morning Prayer. You may wish to sing psalms for which music is available. For subsequent communal psalm prayers, select other psalms from the list above, hymns from your community's hymnal, and scripture readings from the daily lectionary, or as appropriate for the season or occasion. Opening sentences, psalm prayers, prayers of thanksgiving and intercession, and dismissal are adapted from *Daily Prayer* 1987, 150, 213 alt., 240, 280, 86.

Opening Sentences
> Because your love is better than life itself, **my lips will give you praise.**
> I will raise my hands to you in prayer, **and praise you with joy!** (Ps 63:4–5)

Morning Hymn: "Morning Hymn" by David Haas (in
Glory and Praise) or another appropriate hymn

Psalm 117

Psalm Prayer
> Lord God, you have revealed your kindness to all
> people. Gather all nations to yourself, that in all the
> various tongues of the earth one hymn of praise may
> rise to you, through Jesus Christ our Lord. **Amen.**

Psalm 148

Psalm Prayer
> God most high, by your Word you created a won-
> drous universe, and through your Spirit you breathed
> into it your breath of life. Accept creation's hymn of
> praise from our lips, and let the praise that is sung in
> heaven resound in the heart of every creature on
> earth to your glory, Father, Son and Holy Spirit, now
> and forever. **Amen.**

Reading: Ephesians 1:3–14

Silent Reflection (or brief homily)

Gospel Canticle: Canticle of Zechariah (sung or recited
responsorially)

Prayers of Thanksgiving and Intercession
> We praise you, God our creator, for your handiwork
> in shaping and sustaining
> your wondrous creation. Especially we thank you for
> the miracle of life and the wonder of living...
> the particular blessings coming to us in this day...
> the resources of the earth...
> gifts of creative vision and skillful craft...
> the treasure stored in every human life.
> We dare to pray for others, O God who sets us free,
> claiming your love in Jesus Christ for the whole

world, committing ourselves to care for those around
us in his name. Especially we pray for:
those who minister to others...
those who are unable to work today...
those who teach and those who learn...
the church in Europe (or Africa, Asia, Latin America,
    Pacific Islands, or a particular country or region).
Eternal God, our beginning and our end, be our
    starting point and our haven and accompany us in
    this day's journey. May our lives give you praise
    now and forever. **Amen.**

The Lord's Prayer

Concluding Sentences
To God be honor and glory forever! **Amen.**

(1 Tim 1:17)

Bless the Lord. **Amen.**

Psalm 32

1 *Of David. A maskil.*

I

Happy the sinner whose fault is removed,
  whose sin is forgiven.
2 Happy those to whom the LORD imputes no guilt,
  in whose spirit is no deceit.

II

3 As long as I kept silent, my bones wasted away;
  I groaned all the day.
4 For day and night your hand was heavy upon me;
  my strength withered as in dry summer heat.

Selah.

5 Then I declared my sin to you;
  my guilt I did not hide.
I said, "I confess my faults to the LORD,"
  and you took away the guilt of my sin.   *Selah.*

6 Thus should all your faithful pray
  in time of distress.
Though flood waters threaten,
  they will never reach them.
7 You are my shelter; from distress you keep me;
  with safety you ring me round.   *Selah.*

III

8 I will instruct you and show you the way you
  should walk,
  give you counsel and watch over you.
9 Do not be senseless like horses or mules;
  with bit and bridle their temper is curbed,
  else they will not come to you.

IV

10 Many are the sorrows of the wicked,
  but love surrounds those who trust in the LORD.
11 Be glad in the LORD and rejoice, you just;
  exult, all you upright of heart. (RNAB)

Seven

Crying Out to God for Forgiveness of Sin: Penitential Psalms

Whatever became of sin? Karl Menninger asked this question in the title of his important work probing the reality of sin in modern America. In like manner, the penitential psalms invite us to explore human experiences that almost defy categorization. Sometimes we feel unutterably sad or ashamed, and we hardly know how to escape these feelings. Dark thoughts might swirl in our heads about things we wish we had not done, things we could have avoided. Sometimes we injure or even sever a relationship through our actions, and we are at a loss to know how to repair it. At other times we feel as if we are stained or polluted in some way and need to be cleansed. Once in a while we entertain a sense of defeat that we have succumbed to evil forces so strong that we could not overcome them. In another vein, we sometimes reflect on how we would like to have been or to have behaved in a murky situation. Such thoughts can bring both clarity to our situation and foster the hope and desire to behave differently in the future.

Such feelings, thoughts, and actions form part of our common human and spiritual experience. At moments of stress and crisis we may want to cry out to God for help out of our situation. In our society many people and institutions try to alleviate suffering, from the therapist, to the spiritual guide, to church rituals for dealing with sin and guilt. From an ancient culture we also receive valuable and time-tested resources for coping with the sadness of sin. The psalmists of Israel shared the kinds of experiences that many of us know from our own day and created prayers for forgiveness, healing, and wholeness.

Church tradition, from as early as St. Augustine, names seven *penitential psalms:* Psalms 6, 32, 38, 51, 102, 130, and 143. Praying these psalms has long been considered an excellent path to repentance and forgiveness of sin. Pope Pius V appointed these psalms for prayer on Fridays, especially during Lent, and two of these psalms (Psalms 51 and 130) found particular emphasis on Good Friday. Martin Luther considered the penitential psalms very important; his first published work (1517) was a translation and exposition of these psalms.

PSALMS DEALING WITH SIN

Most of us expect Eucharist or Sunday worship service to have a confession of sin or penitential rite at its beginning, usually before the hearing of God's word. Not surprisingly, such expectations tend to structure our view of Christian life: sin, confession, pardon, and then the ability to hear God's word and to live it out in worship and in life. Our experience of sin—both concrete sins and an awareness of sinfulness—is central to the living of Christian life.

Why do we discuss these penitential psalms only after introducing several other types of psalms? More than one-third of the 150 psalms can be described as psalms of lament, calling on God to save us from desperate straits. The penitential psalms, however, number only seven. Some psalms that deal with sin are not penitential; for example, Psalm 36 probes the motivations of sinners, but those sinners are enemies of the psalmist. So the psalter preserves many more psalms crying out to God in human need than psalms in which people cry out to God for forgiveness—perhaps the ratio exceeds six to one! Such numerical comparisons tell only a partial truth, for Israel knew other ways of dealing with the experience of sin, especially through rituals for individuals conducted at a sanctuary or temple, especially if their offenses were not premeditated or intentional (see, for example, Leviticus 4—5). Still, there is much more to be learned about sin and confession from the psalms.

The penitential psalms all present traumatic experiences of suffering, very similar to psalms of lament. These psalms, however, differ from laments in an important way: The psalmist seems convinced that the suffering is caused by sin of some kind. Such feelings should not surprise us—after all, most people think there must be a good reason behind their suffering, that they have done something wrong to deserve it. As Hermann Gunkel wrote in 1933:

> Divine wrath is not without cause. *Sin and guilt* instigate it. It is significant that the Israelite does not present his God as an arbitrary God. YHWH does not act without reason. If the one praying has taken ill, he must recognize in complete contrition that *his offense* has caused YHWH's wrath to spew. The first thing he can do to rid himself of the illness is to set aside its cause, meaning to seek YHWH's forgiveness humbly. (Gunkel 1998, 136)

In our treatment of laments we noted that many of these psalms include a protestation of innocence: "I did nothing to deserve this suffering." In these cases we can look honestly at the situations in which innocent people do suffer. But the penitential psalms focus on the opposite experience: The sufferers do not claim innocence but rather confess their offenses and beg God's forgiveness and help. Psalms of penitence also actually derive from the experience of suffering, but suffering that the psalmist considers deserved. Even when the particular transgression does not seem obvious, the language suggests that God's anger derives from something specific, not a generalized notion of human sinfulness. Protestant Old Testament scholar Claus Westermann finds great help in the psalms when they express sorrow for particular, concrete sins. For him they provide a needed corrective to a common Christian practice of expressing sorrow for a rather vague human sinfulness, whether or not we feel sorrow for anything in particular. Westermann believes that a focus on the general state of sinfulness has so overtaken Western Protestant spirituality that people find it difficult to cry out to God in specific cases. Expressing sorrow for specific offenses is a counterbalance found in the penitential psalms.

How can we be forgiven the sins in our lives? This question has been addressed by people of biblical faith, both Christians and Jews, for many centuries. We wonder how to seek forgiveness from God and from those we have wronged for our public and our private sins. We can find in the psalms some answers to these important questions.

What constitutes genuine sin in our lives? We will find in several psalms a fairly sophisticated analysis of different types of sin. These categories of sin also appear in some of Israel's sacrificial rituals for the Jerusalem Temple. Among the psalms we meet ways of begging God for forgiveness, and these psalms provide a small but important school of prayer for those who recognize a need for healing and forgiveness of particular sins.

LAMENTS OF LOVED SINNERS

In the Book of Psalms sin usually enters the scene through laments, prayers uttered to God for divine help, forgiveness, and assistance. Six of the seven penitential psalms are laments (Psalms 6, 38, 51, 102, 130, 143), while the seventh is a psalm of thanksgiving (Psalm 32). Sin appears within the experience of human suffering and the outpouring to God to alleviate that suffering. Here lies the first and most important point about sin and the psalms: We attend to our sin when its grave consequences push us toward God, asking God to alter our experience of suffering. These psalms focus our attention on one central point: God, and only God, can change this reality in our lives.

Many stories about sin in the Old Testament provide notions of sin for further reflection. Where did sin emerge (Gen 3; Gen 6:1–13)? What does it do to people (Gen 4, 11; 2 Sam 11—12)? How can the effects of sin be reversed (2 Sam 12; Lev 4—5)? Sin in Israel's life shows up in many places in the Bible, but prayers to be relieved of sin in the Book of Psalms remind us that all sin ultimately dislodges or ruptures a relationship with God, and that only God can change that.

These psalms teach us not to ponder our sins in isolation, not to delve into self-judgment. Whenever the psalmists describe sin and its personal impact, they do so relationally, in dialogue with the God who can change things. This God of the psalms and of the covenant desires to repair the broken bonds; it is God's will that humans who have sinned return to God. Sorrow for sin and penitence reach full maturity only in relationship with the loving God of the covenant, who desires more for us than we do for ourselves. Feelings of stain, pollution, defeat, or utter shame cannot stand up against the God of mercy, who is repeatedly invoked in these psalms. A similar approach to sin emerges in a later Christian spirituality, that of the *Spiritual Exercises* of St. Ignatius of Loyola. In the First Week of the *Exercises,* the retreatant ponders his or her sins only in the context of a loving God, who loves us even when we sin. Some have described this as the relationship of a "loved sinner" with God. For Ignatius and for the psalmists, human prayer for forgiveness does not lead to isolation but to communion.

THE PSYCHOLOGY OF SIN IN THE PSALMS

The psalms offer a sophisticated notion of the ways in which sin enters our lives. We use the word *psychology* not as a field of study but to describe various states of the human psyche, as did John Calvin when he said that the psalms contain a complete anatomy of all the states of the soul. Various understandings of sin in the Book of Psalms appear through the different words used to describe this reality. We will discuss a few words that stand out in Psalms 32, 38, and 51.

The psalmists speak of "transgressions" *(pesha),* which are acts of rebellion against legitimate authority, usually against God. We also hear of "sin" *(hatta)* as a faulty action often described metaphorically as "missing the mark," either deliberately or not; in either case it generally injures communal relationships. The speakers also confess "iniquity" *(awon)*, which refers to a crooked, bent, or malformed action; *awon* refers both to the action and also to the effects of the action, such as "guilt" *(awon)*. Many of these terms mirror the different ways that we speak of sin today, each with slightly different experiential connotations.

In Psalm 32 a loved and forgiven sinner thanks God for guidance and forgiveness of sin. This is the only penitential psalm not in the lament genre; the gratitude expressed suggests that God has already responded to the psalmist's cry for mercy. It begins with a proclamation of blessing in verses 1 and 2. "Happy are those who…" is a typical blessing formula. In verses 3–4 the psalmist reminisces about the physical experience of sin, describing the bodily feelings. In verse 5 comes a confession of sin, using the same three words found in verses 1–2: *pesha, hatta,* and *awon*.

1   Happy are those whose *transgression* is forgiven,
        whose *sin* is covered.
2   Happy are those to whom the LORD imputes no
        iniquity,
        and in whose spirit there is no deceit.
3   While I kept silence, my body wasted away
        through my groaning all day long.
4   For day and night your hand was heavy upon
        me;
        my strength was dried up as by the heat of
    summer. *Selah*
5   Then I acknowledged my *sin* to you,
        and I did not hide my *iniquity;*
        I said, "I will confess my *transgressions* to the
        LORD,"
        and you forgave the *guilt of my sin. Selah*

The psalm not only gives a terminology for sin but also describes feelings related to sin: wasting away, groaning, a heavy hand bearing down, withering of strength.

In Psalm 38 the psalmist begs God to let go of divine wrath and uses two of the same words for sin used in Psalm 32: *hatta* and *awon*. Again the psalmist feels the heavy hand of God, but also experiences God's "arrows" sinking into the body.

1   O LORD, do not rebuke me in your anger,
        or discipline me in your wrath.
2   For your arrows have sunk into me,
        and your hand has come down on me.
3   There is no soundness in my flesh
        because of your indignation;
        there is no health in my bones because of my *sin*
4   For my *iniquities* have gone over my head;
        they weigh like a burden too heavy for me.
5   My wounds grow foul and fester because of my
        foolishness....

The psalmist acknowledges foolishness, sin, and iniquity, but in this case does not confess willful rebellion against God.

Psalm 51, often called the *Miserere* (from its opening word in the Latin translation), presents a range of words for sin, including those used in Psalms 32 and 38.

1   Have mercy on me, O God, according to your
        steadfast love;
        according to your abundant mercy blot out
        my *transgressions.*
2   Wash me thoroughly from my *iniquity,*
        and cleanse me from my *sin.*
3   For I know my *transgressions,*
        and my *sin* is ever before me.
4   Against you, you alone, have I *sinned,* and done
        what is evil in your sight,
        so that you are justified in your sentence and
        blameless when you pass judgment.
5   Indeed, I was born *guilty,*
        a sinner when my mother conceived me.

This psalmist begins by begging for God's mercy and forgiveness of sin in verses 1–2 and then repeats these different words for sin in the confession of sin in verses 3–5. Even if we do not connect this psalm with the story of David's sin against Uriah and Bathsheba, we can hear a description of sin: rebelliousness against God that bends right relationships awry and tangles communal relationships. Exploring the impact of a seriously sinful action often reveals most of these effects, each of which disfigures right human and divine relationships.

VOCABULARY FOR SIN

Although we suggested translations for the various Hebrew words above, there really is no standard for translation of these words and their nuances. Carlo Martini suggested different ways of expressing the words and the verbs that accompany them, using Psalm 51:

Hebrew Word	In NRSV	In RNAB	Carlo Martini (Ps 51)
pesha (acts of rebellion against God)	transgression	offense (Ps 51) fault (Ps 32)	cross out my *rebellion*
hatta (a faulty action, "missing the mark," deliberate or not, hurts communal relationships)	sin	sin	cleanse me, "get me out of" all my *transgression*
awon (crooked, bent, or malformed action; refers both to action and the result)	iniquity	guilt	wash me from all my *discord*

Martini combines all these ideas into a description of sin as "the fundamental spoiling of a person. It is a distortion, a disharmony, a rebellion, a will to something other than, and opposed to, the designs of God" (Martini 1992, 84). Sin *(hatta)* in these texts may even be something unintentional or unrecognized, something we would describe not as sin but as an offense or transgression. For example, a person might come into contact with something unclean (Lev 5:2–10); the contact has its effect on relationships and boundaries but can hardly be considered a rebellion. Martini describes it as "transgression," an unintentional action. Perhaps the goal of these different words for sin is not precision but a more inclusive view for people involved in covenantal relationship with God.

We must also attend to God's role in these psalms. God's actions seem much more important than an exploration of sin. The psalmist begins not with an account of sin but with an address to God, begging mercy. God is characterized by mercy and compassion (or abundant mercy) in verse 1. The rich variety of terms for sin finds its match in the ways that God is called to respond: have mercy, blot out, wash thoroughly, cleanse. *Cleanse* usually refers to ceremonial impurities, and here the object of this action is the type of offense that may be willful or not, that may result from contagious contact. The goal of this cleansing is to prevent contagion. To "wash thoroughly" suggests vigorous action, like scrubbing clothes in a river or stream on rocks. "Blot out" seems to have the nuance of erasing from view (cf. Neh 13:14); its objects are the psalmist's rebellious transgressions, which may be the most serious of these types of sin (Stuhlmueller 1983a, 258). In Psalm 51 the psalmist focuses on God and God's actions in the first verse, but then shifts to a confession of sin before returning to God's actions and love.

The first verse of Psalm 51 reveals a God bound by covenant with Israel and with this sinner. This sinner can count on God's graciousness because of the history of the relationship between God and Israel: The NRSV translation of *hesed* as "steadfast love" describes the relationship better than "goodness" in RNAB. But "abundant mercy" in the NRSV translation is better rendered by the RNAB as "abundant compassion," since the Hebrew word *rachamim* really suggests maternal love, the bond between womb and child. We petition God, as we would a mother, to blot out all vestiges of the rebellious activity that threatens to break the relationship of love between us. Prior to the confession of sin, we stand before a lovingly merciful God, and after the soul-searching ceases, this same God is exhorted to fill us with truth, wisdom, joy and gladness, a clean heart, and a spirit of holiness. The psalmist uses a theologically charged word in verse 10: "*Create* in me a clean heart, O God." In the Old Testament only God creates (no other being is ever the subject of this verb, *bara*), so here the psalmist acknowledges that we humans do not have it in our power to cleanse our hearts, to renew our lives. Confession of sin by itself will not bring health and a clean heart, nor will any of the means—either spiritual or psychological—that humans typically employ. Forgiveness of sins occurs only when a merciful God recreates a bond of love with God's creation. Love is stronger than sin or any of sin's effects in our lives.

TWO PENITENTIAL PSALMS

PSALM 6

We discussed the first penitential psalm in the chapter on laments. Someone who is critically ill personally appeals to God for pity, healing, mercy, and to be saved from death. Unlike many lament psalms, we find here no protestation of innocence. Nor does the psalmist confess personal guilt. Perhaps some transgression brought on this sickness, and that is why the psalmist asks God's mercy. This psalm does not speak of the sin of the singer but about its consequences: personal illness (vv. 2–3, 6–7) and social sin, the attacks of enemies (vv. 8–10). The logic of sin, rather than the language of sin, accounts for this psalm's presence among the penitential psalms. Psalm 6 reminds us that our experience of sadness and suffering may derive from the phenomenon of sin in our lives, so we may pray this psalm or one like it for healing and forgiveness.

PSALM 38

This psalm also shows a psalmist suffering from terrible illness, acutely aware that sin provokes God's anger. We noted that the Hebrew words for sin that appear here are "sin" and "iniquity" but not "rebellion." If we pay particular attention to the physical symptoms bewailed by the psalmist in vv. 2–3, 5–8, 10, such as foul and festering sores indicative of some kind of skin disease, the connection between sin and illness is clear in this psalm.

The psalmist seems burdened by a number of sins and transgressions and believes they have brought on illness, abandonment, hostility, depression. In recent decades the

suffering of people with the AIDS virus parallels the
dilemma of this psalmist. Those afflicted with HIV or
AIDS often struggle with abandonment by friends, relatives, and even members of their church communities.
This psalm poignantly records the emotions of one who
experiences not only the pain of illness but rejection and
the loss of significant relationships. It also acknowledges
the common feeling that sin causes illness and suffering,
even though we know the relationship between sin and
suffering is far more complex. It is important to maintain
the distinction between personal sin and illness.

Finally, this confession is not without hope: The
psalmist confidently begs God's love and mercy many
times (vv. 1, 9, 15, 16, 21, 22), and the psalm concludes
with the hope-filled words: "Lord, my salvation."
"Salvation" does not suggest only a spiritual transition; it
most often connotes God's saving activities for Israel, saving them in battle from their enemies. This psalmist hopes
in the God who can and does save people. Finally, we
return to an earlier observation about the words for sin in
this psalm. The notion of rebellious activity against God is
conspicuously absent. In a psalm filled with imagery of
horrible illness, the idea of deliberate sin is not found.
Sometimes we tend to blame victims of serious illnesses
because we consider their faults, failings, and sins so
severe. But this psalm raises a question: Has the sick person indeed sinned so grievously? Still, this psalmist ends
with hope in the God of salvation.

PSALMS OF PENITENCE AND THE LIFE OF FAITH

David stands out in the Hebrew scriptures as a model of repentance. Who can forget the way that the prophet Nathan confronts him for sexually exploiting Bathsheba and arranging the death of her husband, Uriah the Hittite? The narrator in 2 Samuel 11 relates the sordid story, with all its evasions and subtle contortions of right relations, including the cynical and ironic way in which Uriah is placed in the position of carrying his own death warrant back to the field commander. In the following chapter the prophet confronts the king; with a subtle parable he tricks David into declaring the heinous nature of a crime like his, and Nathan proclaims: "You are the man." David's repentance is grand and sincere, and as a result God spares his life, though not that of the child. But David's honest, forthright acceptance of divine judgment marks him forever as a great example of humble repentance.

It comes as no surprise that five of the seven penitential psalms are connected with David in their superscriptions: Psalms 6, 32, 38, 51, and 143. The most famous of these is Psalm 51, and its superscription explicitly connects the psalm with David's most notable sin: "A Psalm of David, when the prophet Nathan came to him, after he had gone in to Bathsheba." Since these psalm titles probably were added later by the Jewish community, we cannot say for certain that David prayed or wrote this psalm, or if he did, at what point in his life. But when Jews in the postexilic era prayed this psalm, it reminded them so much of the way they imagined David's experience and his repentance that they connected this psalm with that event. They found a time and an event in David's life for the spirituality expressed in this psalm. When we recite or pray this psalm and think of the gravity of David's offense—adultery and murder to hide the evidence—we can transfer the sentiments and prayer to our own situation, especially when we feel burdened by sin. Most striking is the clear admission that in harming Uriah and Bathsheba, David has sinned against God. All of them are in covenantal relationship with God, so harm to other covenant partners constitutes sin against God. In the narrative God forgives David, but the effects of his actions continue to plague his royal household. Absalom kills Amnon in revenge. So begins Absalom's rebellion against his father and the continual suffering of the family and everyone connected to it (2 Samuel 13—20). This ongoing saga suggests the monumental impact of sinful actions, even when the sin is forgiven by God.

The psalm teaches us how to pray in similarly bleak situations in our own lives. It appears often in Christian prayer books; for example, in the Roman Liturgy of the Hours people pray this psalm each Friday morning. Carlo Martini reminds us of the great importance of Psalm 51 throughout the history of Christian spirituality. It stands at the core of Augustine's *Confessions* and was very important for the meditation and prayer of Gregory the Great. Joan of Arc's soldiers used it as a battle cry; Martin Luther wrote unforgettable passages on it; and Bach, Donizetti, and others conveyed its spirituality in music (Martini 1992, 83).

In medieval England many writers portrayed David as the perfect example "of compunction or penitential humility, citing and commenting on the Psalms in order to induce a humble attitude in their hearers" (Kuczynski 1995, 84). Of course, Psalms 51 and 32 were favorites of these spiritual writers. The same is true for Middle English poetry. With these writers and many others "we can make our own the prayer of Charles de Foucauld: 'O God, I thank you for giving us that divine prayer, the *Miserere*'" (Martini 1992, 83).

God is the actor whom we beg to change our lives, not only by forgiving us but also by transforming us: "Create in me a clean heart, O God, and put a new and right spirit within me" (Ps 51:10). When the one who prays experiences forgiveness, then public praise of God is the outcome: "My tongue will sing aloud of your deliverance" (Ps 51:14b). This promise of a psalm of thanksgiving prompted a search for such a psalm, and many have considered Psalm 32 to be David's response to God's graciousness and forgiveness. These two penitential psalms, one a lament and the other a thanksgiving psalm, offer rich fare for our own meditation and prayer.

Appropriating Penitential Psalms for Our Lives

Sin is a difficult and confusing reality to talk and pray about. One difficulty occurs if we focus on ourselves as wretched sinners in such a way that we systematically undermine our sense of ourselves as God's new creation (2 Cor 5:17). But a very different outcome is possible when we are able to focus, concretely and specifically, on actions or omissions by which we have harmed others and ruptured our relationship with God. The penitential psalms focus more on the latter, so praying the penitential psalms makes great spiritual and psychological sense at those moments when we are overwhelmed by the realization of our own sin. But can these psalms become a regular part of our prayer? Should they? On what grounds?

Many persons avoid reflecting on sinfulness, banishing it from their consciousness. Others ignore personal sin but dwell on the sinfulness of humankind. Still others, probably many more than we realize, find that guilt over their sin or humankind's sinful condition hovers constantly at the edges of their consciousness. Perhaps both those who banish sinfulness from their consciousness and those who are consumed by it suffer from the same malady—they are unable to experience themselves as loved by God just as they are, sins and all. Regular prayer with the penitential psalms can address just this reality. Penitential psalms, without exception, reveal that humankind and God are in a covenantal relationship, which God maintains no matter what we do. Sometimes a psalm notes that God has promised something the psalmist has not yet experienced, but always there is the sense that God *will* have mercy. God's mercy and compassion are everlasting to those who love God. Luke reminds us of the same message in his parable of the good shepherd: "I tell you there will be more joy in heaven over one sinner who repents than over ninety-nine righteous persons who need no repentance" (Luke 15:7). Our sin and our sinful condition draw us back again into the arms of the covenental, compassionate God, who can and does change our lot.

To summarize: The penitential psalms provide us a way to deal with our sin, leading neither to solipsistic attack on ourselves nor to systematic evasion of our responsibilities. These psalms beckon us into energetic dialogue with the God of the covenant, who in turn names our sin, forgives our sin, and through it all continues to love us. Penitential psalms revolve around earnest petitions to God—for healing, for forgiveness—and grateful responses for God's intervention. And they allow God to teach us anew and continually that we are truly loved sinners in God's eyes.

PRAYING PENITENTIAL PSALMS

EXAMINATION OF CONSCIOUSNESS THROUGH A PSALM

Psalm 32 (ICEL 1994) provides the structure for this guided meditation on our true self before God.

• Allow yourself to become aware of your relationships: with yourself, with others, especially your loved ones, and, ultimately, with God....In this context hear the words of the psalmist: "Happy the pardoned...whose sin is canceled...in whom God finds no evil, no deceit."

• Rest here. Let the sense of promise contained in these words take root within you.

• Recall a past experience of being forgiven. Remember the lightness, the joy, the "at-one-ness" that filled you. Ask again for this grace.

• Our sinful condition is seldom easy for us to face. It is too embarrassing, too debilitating, too discouraging: "While I hid my sin, my bones grew weak from endless groaning."

• Allow yourself to stay with your hidden sinfulness for some minutes, inviting God to surface what God wishes you to see about yourself: "Then I stopped hiding my sin and spoke out, 'God, I confess my wrong.' And you pardoned me."

• Express your sorrow to God, for our God is forever merciful.

• Receive God's pardon now: "You, my shelter, you save me from ruin. You encircle me with songs of freedom."

• Receive God's freedom into your deepest self. God says: "I show you the path to walk. As your teacher, I watch out for you."

• Hear God's promise to lead you.

• Offer thanks to God for renewing, once again, God's covenant with you: "Rejoice in the Lord. Be glad and sing, you faithful and just."

• For we know from whom comes our faithfulness and justice. Blessed be God our Redeemer! Amen.

AN EXAMINATION OF CONSCIENCE

Some of us examine our conscience by reflecting on the Ten Commandments or the Beatitudes, noting how our lives have or have not measured up to these scriptural descriptions of right living. Several psalms (such as Psalms 15 and 24:3–6) and Isaiah 33:13–16 functioned in pre-exilic Israel in a strikingly similar way.

• Read Psalm 15 very slowly, touching the various aspects of your life against the values and actions that this psalm teaches as necessary for those coming into God's house, God's holy mountain. Express sorrow for those areas of your life that do not reflect these values. Ask God to forgive your actions and omissions and to deepen these values, attitudes, and actions within you.

• Some other psalms concern disregard for the covenant with God and may suggest further issues for self and communal examination; Psalms 50, 81, and 82 fall into this category.

LECTIO DIVINA WITH A PENITENTIAL PSALM

One penitential psalm in particular, Psalm 51, has become a testament not only to the human propensity for sin but also to God's predilection for forgiving the repentant one. This psalm has become traditional for Fridays, reminding us regularly of our continual need for forgiveness.

• Select a translation of Psalm 51 to which you feel drawn. Read the psalm aloud slowly, several times. Or, sing it in one of the hymn settings available to you. Notice whether it contains all the psalm verses and sentiments.

• Allow the movements of *lectio divina* to flow in and out of each other for as long as they are lively, or for the length of time that you have set aside for prayer.

• At the conclusion of the *lectio divina* period, note in your journal what happened; for example, the word or phrase(s) you focused on, some of the ruminations or insights that came to you, the core of your response of God, and the "tone" of the contemplative moment.

You may wish to return to the same psalm each Friday for a number of weeks, allowing the repetition to carry you deeper in the same direction, or into a new place in the same psalm. Or select another of the penitential psalms and repeat the *lectio* process. How does your prayer shift over the weeks? Your sense of yourself? of God?

HANDMADE MIDRASH

• Select another penitential psalm, or continue working with Psalm 51. Review a commentary on your chosen psalm. Reflect on the psalm (perhaps through *lectio divina*), and state the essence that you will express visually.

• Using a simple medium that allows color, such as crayons, paints, colored pens or pencils on white paper, express this essence. Do not try to make figures that obviously portray someone or something. Allow the forms and colors to arise spontaneously.

• Discuss the resulting creation with one other person. Pay particular attention to the role of color. The suggested questions in chapter 2 may prove helpful.

• Write in your journal, noting how the sense of opposites within the psalm and within you might have shifted in the process of creating the midrash. See the questions in chapter 2.

• Reflect: How does the psalm now speak to, of, or for
you? to, of, or for God?

EXPRESSING PENITENTIAL PSALMS IN MOVEMENT

• Select a simple, easily repeated movement to express
penitence, such as striking your breast, making a deep
bow, or extending your hands in supplication. Now decide
upon a simple gesture that expresses forgiveness and reconciliation, such as clasped hands, hands folded across
your breast or upraised with palms upturned. Pray Psalm
32 with these gestures. Or simply pray Psalm 32, letting
your body express it as you pray.

SINGING THE PENITENTIAL PSALMS

• Select a penitential psalm setting. Sing it several times
until it has impressed itself upon you. Try to memorize
part of the psalm in this musical setting and sing it (interiorly or aloud) throughout the day. Or create a simple tune
to several verses of a penitential psalm. Artistic value is
not the goal; rather, seek to embody the psalm through the
medium of your voice.

Psalm	Title	Tune/Composer	Hymnal
32	Steadfast Love	Diemer	NCH
51	Have Mercy, Lord	Gelineau	G
51	Create in Me a Clean Heart	Francke	WOV
102	O Lord, Hear My Prayer	Berthier (Taizé)	G, WOV
130	Out of the Depths	Aus Tiefer Not	PH, UMH, HER, LBW

| 130 | Out of the Depths I Call | St. Bride CM | NCH, NEC |
| 143 | When Morning Lights the Eastern Sky | St. Stephen CM | PH |

CORPORATE PSALM PRAYER: SERVICE OF RECONCILIATION

The following service is designed for a group to express its sorrow for wrongs committed and to receive forgiveness from God. It should be adapted to your community's situation and tradition, using familiar hymns, adding sacramental confession, or leaving time for silent confession, adding assurance of pardon, and so on.

Opening Hymn: "There's a Wideness in God's Mercy" *(In Babilone)* or another hymn

Greeting

The grace of Jesus Christ and the love of God and the peace of the Holy Spirit be with you all. **And also with you.**

From the depths I call to you, Lord, hear my cry. **Catch the sound of my voice raised up, pleading.**

If you record our sins, Lord, who could survive? **But because you forgive we stand in awe.** (Ps 130:1–4, ICEL 1994)

Opening Prayer

Holy God, your Word, Jesus Christ, spoke peace to a sinful world and brought humankind the gift of reconciliation by his life, suffering, death, and resurrection. Teach all who bear his name to follow the example he gave us. May our faith, hope, and love turn hatred to love, conflict to peace, and death to eternal life, through Christ our Lord. **Amen.**

First Reading: Micah 7:18–20 or 2 Corinthians 5:17–21

Responsorial Psalm: Psalm 51

Gospel: Matthew 9:9–13

Homily (or silent reflection)

Sung Response: "Kyrie Eleison," Jacques Berthier (Taizé)

Confession (individual, where appropriate, or silent) Followed by Assurance of Pardon

Response: "Blest Be the Lord" (Psalm 91) by Dan Schutte or another appropriate hymn

Concluding Blessing (extend hands over one another)
May the God who is slow to anger and abounding in kindness shed merciful light upon us. May God surround us with compassion and love. May God enlighten us so that we may walk in justice and truth all our days. May God bless us and keep us now and forever. Amen.

Sign of Peace

Psalm 128

1   A song of ascents.

I
Happy are all who fear the LORD,
   who walk in the ways of God.
2   What your hands provide you will enjoy;
   you will be happy and prosper;
3   Like a fruitful vine
   your wife within your home,
Like olive plants
   your children around your table.
4   Just so will they be blessed
   who fear the LORD.

II
5   May the Lord bless you from Zion,
   all the days of your life
That you may share Jerusalem's joy
6   and live to see your children's children.
Peace upon Israel! (RNAB)

Eight
Wondering at God's Ways: Wisdom Psalms

Most of the psalms we have presented had some type of ritual or liturgical focus in Israel's life, so they remind us of life at a sanctuary or in the Jerusalem Temple. But most people spend the bulk of their time at home or in the marketplace, engaged in everyday matters and relationships. They concern themselves with struggles over how to succeed, how to maintain homes and families, how to mend broken relationships, and how to achieve harmony with friends and relatives. The more daily aspects of human existence evoke a different kind of response and literature, often called *wisdom literature*. Here God is not absent but is clearly experienced in different ways and moods.

The wisdom movement was present throughout the whole Ancient Near East, and it influenced Israel quite early. Solomon became known for his wisdom, and, as happens so frequently in the Bible, wise sayings are attributed to Solomon to locate them in the "authority" of that tradition. This practice may explain the traditional connection of Solomon with the Books of Proverbs and Ecclesiastes. With the so-called wisdom psalms, we enter a somewhat different mindset than the world of Israel's history and worship.

WISDOM ROOTED IN THE GOODNESS OF CREATION

The goodness of God's creation provides a basic presupposition for wisdom literature and psalms. In the first account of creation (Gen 1:1—2:4b) each "day" of the creation week has a special pattern. God's intention ("let there be...") is followed by divine action to bring about that goal. Afterward, from the third through the sixth days, God looked at what had been created that day and saw that "it was good." The Hebrew word for "good" *(tov)* has an aesthetic connotation, signaling the pleasing beauty and harmony of God's creation. Enjoying the goodness of creation corresponds to the experience of prosperity, and some wisdom psalms envisage this kind of "good" as desirable. In Psalm 128:5 the NRSV translates the word *tov* concretely: "May you see the *prosperity* of Jerusalem." Earlier in that same psalm a different way of describing prosperity (well-being) also derives from this same word: for those who fear the LORD "it shall go *well* with you" (Ps 128:2). Another psalm connects generous and just behavior with well-being: "It is *well* with those who deal generously and lend, who conduct their affairs with justice" (Ps 112:5). The goodness of God's creation was intended for all God's creatures, especially human beings.

The goal of wisdom, then, is simple: the good life. Various threads of the wisdom tradition, however, vary in their content: training of kings and royal counselors, nature wisdom, theological wisdom, and experiential wisdom—the largest category. Experiential wisdom is an attempt to understand and cope with the complete environment. In proverbial wisdom, especially, successful insights are captured in pithy sayings that could easily be passed on in an oral culture—a ready and effective way of teaching children the accumulated wisdom of the community. We still do it today, citing such proverbs as "Pride goeth before the fall" (Murphy 1968, 447–48).

WISDOM AS THE ABILITY TO LIVE "THE GOOD LIFE"

The wisdom tradition preserves much pragmatic musing such as "this is how to live if you want to know the good life." The sayings were gathered together under the name of a famous teacher and passed on as an effective means of socialization. Wisdom does not come simply from observing human conduct or through rational reflection on the teaching handed down in the wisdom schools. Rather, for Israel, "the beginning" (that is, the foundation, the premise) of wisdom is *faith* in Yahweh (Anderson 2000, 187). Israel put its own stamp on this tradition.

Israel's sages believed that actions have consequences. They based this belief on a theology of creation: God made creatures a certain way. If we follow that order of creation, we will be happy; if we transgress it, we will not reap the benefits. If these results don't come now, they will come later. But here we stumble upon one of the difficulties in some of the wisdom psalms: In order to have enough "later" for just people to be vindicated, we have to leave this life and find the reward in a next world—precisely what the psalmists didn't believe. Later wisdom writers reflected on retribution after death, especially for righteous sufferers: in the Book of Daniel and the Wisdom of Solomon, the authors ponder the resurrection of the just and immortality of the soul as ways of vindicating suffering.

The psalms are more optimistic than other strains of wisdom literature; they insist that God's *torah* ("teaching," "command," "instruction"—often poorly and rigidly translated as "law") will reveal how to live in harmony. In Psalm 112 (page 188), we observe the goodness of life but also notice how closely tied are wisdom and justice, qualities desperately needed today.

If we want to pass on to our children what we have found valuable from our experiences and education, how might we do so? The short, pithy proverb is one way. "Don't count your chickens before they're hatched" is one that many of us have internalized. Another way is through provocative stories, those with a twist, which worm their way into our consciousness precisely because they can't be pinned down to one meaning. Jesus used the parable form from the wisdom tradition extensively. Another way might be to tell stories about people who embody the values that we want to pass on. Family stories often immortalize a relative and teach a value to the next generation. Another way is to create ideal types—we probably learned what a good mother or a good father is through a version of family storytelling. The last chapter of Proverbs, 31:10–31, speaks of an ideal woman in just this manner. Incidentally, notice the echoes in the family described in Psalm 112.

Everyday wisdom in the Bible leads us to wonder how to relate to others, to society, and to God. We might consider it an attempt to garner relational wisdom and a style of life. It allows us to ponder home and marketplace, family relations and workplace situations. When Kathleen O'Connor speaks of wisdom for the marketplace, she thinks not only of public life and actions but of everything that constitutes elements of a good and happy life, including food, clothing, and other necessities of life as well as harmonious and neighborly actions (O'Connor 1988, 13–14).

THE "GOOD LIFE" IN WISDOM PSALMS

Several psalms invite us to ponder the rewarding joys of life from the vantage point of family and everyday life. Psalm 127 seems to draw on ancient proverbial sayings:

> 1 Unless the LORD builds the house, those who build it labor in vain.
> Unless the LORD guards the city, the guard keeps watch in vain.
> 2 It is in vain that you rise up early and go late to rest, eating the bread of anxious toil;
> for he gives sleep to his beloved.

Far from endorsing a laid-back or lazy style of life, this psalmist reflects on the folly of excessive human effort unless one is involved with God. But these lines may say more about God than about humans—that it is God who builds, defends, and gives rest (sleep). The "house" that God builds may also involve a play on words. The Hebrew word refers both to the building and the family that dwells there. With this pun the psalmist reminds hearers that a family grows only by God's involvement, by God "building the house." The second part of the psalm takes up a similar motif: "Sons are indeed a heritage from the LORD, the fruit of the womb a reward" (v. 3). As Stuhlmueller points out, this psalm hints that wisdom includes "looking to God as their creator and sustainer of life," which may have led to the custom of singing this psalm to celebrate the birth of a new baby (Stuhlmueller 1983b, 166).

Psalm 128 also celebrates the gift of family as a reward for the wise, for those who "fear the LORD." The perspective is that of the male.

3   Your wife will be like a fruitful vine within your
      house;
      your children will be like olive shoots around
      your table.
4   Thus shall the man be blessed who fears the
      LORD.

But children are not the only blessing of those who walk
in God's ways. They shall also reap the benefit of their
hard work: "You shall eat the fruit of the labor of your
hands; you shall be happy and it will go well with you" (v.
2). Because it mentions labor and its fruit, the rabbis often
extolled the dignity of good, honest work from this verse
(Cohen 1945, 430). Another meaning might also be envis-
aged: Those who fear God will actually enjoy the fruit of
their labors rather than turning the bulk of it over in tax-
ation or payment to wealthy landowners. In two distinct
ways family life will be blessed for those who live in
accord with wisdom.

In Psalm 128 the benefits are not confined to the realm
of the family and its life. The blessing at the conclusion of
this psalm also expands to encompass all of Jerusalem (v.
5) and even Israel (v. 6). For this psalmist the blessing
comes not only to the powerful and people of status but
also to ordinary families, even peasants. Wisdom also gifts
those in simple circumstances, promising something many
people would love to experience: "May you see your children's children. Peace be upon Israel!" (v. 6). In a subtle
fashion the psalm intertwines the blessings of a good life
at the level of people, city, and family. Peace *(shalom)* and
prosperity *(tob)* stand together as hope and promise for
people of wisdom.

Psalm 133 begins on a lovely note: "How very good
and pleasant it is when kindred live together in unity!" (v.
1). The psalmist compares this joy to the experience of
precious oil on the head "running down upon the beard"

or to the delicate beauty of "the dew of Hermon" (vv. 2, 3). Older translations had a familial ring: "when brothers dwell in unity" (v. 1b, RSV). If one thinks of family, a social setting where differences can run wide and deep, this psalm rejoices in harmonious family relations. In addition, it was one of Israel's pilgrimage psalms, and some commentators reflect on the unifying experience of pilgrims journeying together. From a historical perspective, this psalm may come from the time of Nehemiah, who tried to rebuild and strengthen the city of Jerusalem after the return from the exile; the psalmist may envision a concentrated and settled population in Jerusalem as a way to invigorate the entire country of Judea (Cohen 1945, 439). Whether one imagines kindred dwelling together in unity or the whole people, the blessings that the psalm promises offer a happy vision of shared life, truly one of wisdom's goals.

Returning again to Psalm 112, we see that the opening line reminds us of hymns of praise: "Praise the LORD!" But then its type changes with the first full verse: "Happy are those who fear the LORD, who greatly delight in his commandments." "Fear of the LORD" reminds us of the wisdom in Proverbs, while "delight in his commandments" reminds us of the joy of Torah. Their lives are characterized by concern to preserve life and to care for the less fortunate: "It is well with those who deal generously and lend, who conduct their affairs with justice" (v. 5) and "They have distributed freely, they have given to the poor" (v. 9a). Various images of blessing (wealth, riches, stability, steadiness, courage) weave around these descriptions of just and wise persons, but a high point emerges in verse 4: "They are gracious, merciful and righteous." All of these adjectives describe God in Exodus 34:6, a text that extols God's outgoing, outpouring love. Here the people whose lives follow the invitation of wisdom and Torah literally imitate

God. One can know God's life by the way of life of these people. What a blessing for those who love wisdom!

In the psalms that we surveyed, the goodness of God's creation stands as the paramount image. Wisdom seeks the good life. Harmony and order exist not only in the universe but also in human interactions, especially in family settings (Pss 127, 128). "Fear of the LORD" characterizes the person who discerns and trusts God's plan for life on earth and relations between humans; those who follow this path live wisely (Ps 128:4). Living wisely, in the fear of the Lord, leads to good life in community with others (Ps 133). Living wisely also leads to concern to preserve life, especially of the less fortunate (Ps 112). Truly the wisdom psalms allow and invite us to celebrate the goodness of life and to strive to ensure it for ourselves and for others.

WHEN THE "GOOD LIFE" ELUDES US

Life frequently does not work out as neatly as the first group of wisdom psalms suggests. How often do people hear the reassuring words that open Psalm 128—"Happy are all who fear the LORD, who walk in the ways of God," RNAB—but feel that they enjoy few of the blessings promised: children and grandchildren, joy, prosperity, and shalom. Instead, they experience illness, privation, poverty, and alienation within society. Written in larger strokes are the complaints and questions of the Book of Job: Why does the just person suffer? Spiritual director Pierre Wolff has written a prayer guide, *May I Hate God?* (1979), to assist people with these nagging questions. And the stunning popularity of Harold Kushner's book *When Bad Things Happen to Good People* (1989) reminds us how much the problem of evil affects people today. Many theologians have discussed the problem under the term *theodicy*, which implies proving God, or proving divine justice, in spite of contrary evidence. The problem of evil in the lives of good and decent people looms as large today as it ever did.

The Book of Psalms includes at least three compositions that probe the insistent questions of the suffering just person: Psalms 37, 49 and 73. In these psalms answers and advice are offered, questions are raised repeatedly, past experiences—both positive and negative—are cited, and God's justice is defended. Poignant suffering is no stronger in these psalms than in some of the lament psalms of the suffering just, such as Psalms 31 and 69. But there is a difference. While lamenters address their questions directly to God ("Why?" "How long?"), these psalms invite discussion, proofs, theological reflection, and dialogue with fellow travelers in faith. Here suffering raises questions about the structure of the cosmos created by God, while in laments the questions turn into demands directed to God, the covenant partner. These psalms have a rather detached feel and so may provide an easier entryway for sufferers who are not prepared to address God so boldly, not ready to turn from intellectual reflection and discussion to direct address.

The traditional answer to the problem of evil shines forth in Psalm 37. As Robert Davidson comments, the author of this psalm "would have been happy with the theology of Job's friends" (1998, 127), those who persistently argued that he must have deserved his sufferings. The opening four verses summarize teaching as contemporary as it is ancient.

> 1 Do not fret because of the wicked;
>   do not be envious of wrongdoers,
> 2 for they will soon fade like the grass,
>   and wither like the green herb.

3 Trust in the LORD, and do good;
       so you will live in the land, and enjoy security.
4 Take delight in the LORD
       and he will give you the desires of your heart.

These lines contain images fruitful for contemplation: The fading grass and the withering herbs are stark reminders that the prosperity of evil persons will not endure. Part of the psalmist's strategy is to let strong images of injustice permeate this psalm. In verses 12, 14, 17, 21, and 35 we hear the evil actions of the wicked described. But each of these cases of wickedness finds retribution in the next verses, and the psalmist connects the "good life" with just actions in even more places: verses 11, 17, 18, 19, 22a, 25, 28–31, 33, 37, and 39–40. The commands in this psalm are directed to fellow Israelites, not to God, as in the laments. Some of them are memorable, worthy of pondering, praying, and living.

5 Commit your way to the LORD;
       trust in him and he will act.
7 Be still before the LORD, and wait patiently for
       him;
       do not fret over those who prosper in their
       way,
       over those who carry out evil devices.
8 Refrain from anger and forsake wrath.
       Do not fret—it leads only to evil.
27 Depart from evil, and do good;
       so you shall abide forever.
34 Wait for the LORD, and keep to his way,
       and he will exalt you to inherit the land....

John Craghan identifies the real focus of this psalm as "the problem of social justice" and suggests that we imagine the speaker as an older sage addressing a young audience about the anomalies, inequities, and atrocities that face its generation (Craghan 1985, 83). The psalmist offers a consoling reflection from a lifetime of experience:

> 25 I have been young, and now am old,
>   yet I have not seen the righteous forsaken
>   or their children begging for bread.
> 26 They are ever giving liberally and lending,
>   and their children become a blessing.

We can protest that such positive outcomes are far too infrequent. We can list the exceptions to this reflection. Yet we might also try to recall experiences in our lives and those of others that buttress the psalmist's trust and confidence in God. Many commentators suggest a connection between wisdom's view—that the fates of the just and wicked shall be reversed—and the Beatitudes of Jesus that Christians know so well (Craghan 1985, 84).

Psalms 49 and 73 explore feelings about the apparent prosperity of the wicked enunciated by those who suffer. In each case the psalmist denies that wealth is a true measure of blessing for the wise and just person. Psalm 49 repeats in various ways that death will provide the final leveling between just and wicked:

> 17 When [the rich] die they will carry nothing
>   away;
>   their wealth will not go down after them.

In Psalm 73 the speaker admits feelings of great envy toward the prosperous:

> 3 For I was envious of the arrogant;
>   I saw the prosperity of the wicked.

In vivid language the psalmist probes their lives (especially vv. 4–12) and concludes that the innocent and just life is lived in vain (vv. 13–14). But unlike the speakers of Psalms

37 and 49, this singer apparently entered the sanctuary with these burning questions. Everything had

> seemed to me a wearisome task
> 17 until I went into the sanctuary of God;
> then I perceived [the wickeds'] end.

Davidson suggests that "through worship, probably through sharing in one of the great festivals of the Hebrew religious year, he was gripped by two convictions": that the fate of the wicked comes without expectation and that the psalmist is guided by God and can let go bitterness of heart (1998, 234).

While Psalms 37 and 49 seem to mirror dialogue and debate, even theological reflection and discussion, the speaker in Psalm 73 pinpoints a resolution in a worship setting. All three psalms offer distinct possibilities for reflection on the problems and ambiguities of our lives and times.

LADY WISDOM: WISDOM PERSONIFIED

Wisdom in the Book of Psalms draws heavily on the perspective of men in society; even when the psalmists focus on the blessings and joys of family life, their vantage point usually is the man's. But Israel recognized other strains of wisdom as divine gifts and celebrated them with beautiful images and hymns. The writer of the Book of Exodus portrays the midwives who saved the Hebrew boys as bearers of wisdom: "But the midwives feared God; they did not do as the king of Egypt commanded them, but they let the boys live" (Exod 1:17). Fear of God usually suggests wisdom, and concern to preserve life often is the goal of women considered wise. In other stories the wise woman of Tekoa acted to save the life of Absalom (2 Samuel 14), while the wise woman of Beth-maacah saved her city from slaughter (2 Sam 20:14–22).

The "wise woman" had made her appearance early in Israel's history, but her concerns were not overtly political. Rather, she strove to preserve the lives of the weak or the innocent. In this respect feminine wisdom truly learned her values from the life of the family and network of relationships in the extended family and village. So we should not be surprised when feminine ways of relating with God and with other humans manifest themselves as gifts of divine Wisdom. This new perspective took concrete shape in Proverbs 1—9.

Who is the Wisdom Woman, Lady Wisdom? Here she seems to be compared with God, to be a mediator between God and humans, for to ignore her counsel is to abandon fear of the Lord (Prov 1:29–30). She is a precious gift, the key to long life, security, and peace (Prov 3:13–18). She is the Lord's instrument at the creation of the world (Prov 3:19–20). She is to be sought after as one's lover and spouse (Prov 4:1–9). Wisdom is to be one's sister or friend (Prov 7:4). She meets people on roads, crossroads, in city gates and approaches to the city (Prov 8:1–3) not only in a religious location or in worship. She prepares a wonderful banquet that brings long life to those who partake of her delights (Prov 9:1–6, 11). Wisdom in these passages in Proverbs entices and befriends, cautions and cares for people as sister, friend, or lover, and since she relates both to God and to human beings, she mediates their mutual relations. She brings joy and celebration to human life.

Perhaps the most exalted wisdom hymn is that of Proverbs 8:22–31. Here Wisdom's existence is traced back to the time of creation, to a bond with God the creator. She is firstborn of God's ways, the forerunner of God's prodigies (v. 22). She was poured forth and present at the beginning of God's creation of the world (vv. 23–29), and she was present as God's master worker and delight, "playing before him always" (v. 30). She delights in human beings and in God's inhabited world (v. 31). Truly Lady Wisdom communicates a different way of relating to Israel's God, a path that opens up many possibilities for spirituality today.

The Book of Proverbs concludes with a text that sometimes proves distasteful to women, due in part to translation issues. In Proverbs 31:10–31 the poet describes a strong and valiant woman who binds together all her relations (children and husband) into a healthy, loving, living unit. Many translations simply speak of her as "the good wife," but we can responsibly translate those same words from the Hebrew as "the valiant woman." The poet may very well be suggesting more than the qualities of a dutiful wife, that this personified wisdom woman reveals qualities of relationality and love in everyday life. The very last verse names a woman's reward as similar to that of the man in Psalm 128:2: "Give her a share in the fruit of her hands, and let her works praise her in the city gates" (Prov 31:31).

How can people embody this kind of spirituality? Not surprisingly, people occasionally choose this text as a scripture reading for their mother's funeral, relishing the many images of motherly wisdom and love in the poem. Perhaps a brief story will hint at another aspect of the wisdom woman's spirituality. One Sister of the Holy Names died of cancer at age fifty-four in Seattle. She was a robust woman, with a hearty laugh and a great smile for everyone. In her final years she worked in an inner-city parish in Seattle, where she was much loved. Huge crowds came for her wake and vigil service, and a lively party followed, just as she would have wished. Her memorial card contained two quotations from Proverbs. One proclaimed: "I was by God's side…delighting God day after day, ever at play in God's presence, at play everywhere in the world, delighting to be with God's people" (Prov 8:30–31). This seemed to capture part of her self-identity before God. The other quotation allowed the rest of us to reflect on her life: "She is clothed in strength and dignity, she can laugh at the days to come. Give her a share in what her hands have worked for, and let her works tell her praises" (Prov 31:25, 31). One who celebrates God's creation, who delights in God's people, who lives life fully and generously embodies a kind of wisdom that God wishes to offer to our world today.

Finally, Lady Wisdom invites us to her house for a banquet ("my bread and…the wine I have mixed") that leads to insight and life (Prov 9:1–6). The rich fare suggests to us not only a way of living, a wisdom spirituality as illustrated in the previous story, it also opens a door for new and surprising images and names for God, the source of wisdom. Wisdom shares divine life as mediator between God and humans, and this analogy with a valiant and loving woman provides new angles for viewing and perceiving God. This metaphor, Wisdom as divine companion, lived on in various new appearances. While New Testament writers described Jesus with wisdom terminology and later church traditions occasionally considered Mary as Seat of Wisdom, some medieval mystics such as Hildegard of Bingen addressed God as Wisdom. In each era wisdom personified as feminine has helped people to imagine God in different ways and to address God with different names and metaphors. Wisdom in the psalms and in other wisdom literature certainly provides new images with which to view our spiritual lives but also gives us new possibilities for theology as we name and describe God in poetic freshness.

Wisdom psalms and hymns invite us to rejoice in the goodness of God's creation, to trust that its blessings come from a wise and skillful Creator, who ordered the cosmos in a pleasing and practical fashion. Daily life, family, relationships, proper behavior, and appreciation of human intellect and artistic sensibilities all constitute gifts from this God; none of them should be summarily despised, even by ascetics. Fear of God shows the beginning of wisdom, but it should also lead to blessing and prosperity. When disaster comes without explanation, some wisdom psalms push the issue of theodicy. The wisdom psalms take seriously the problems that arise when life's goodness seems absent and evil is flourishing. Sometimes they advise sufferers to keep a steady course (Ps 37), at other times they promise that just people will eventually experience blessing (Ps 49), and one psalmist exclaims that his struggles and complaints were transformed in a worship experience (Ps 73).

Finally, these psalms and the hymns in Israel's wisdom literature remind us that wisdom lodges in the lives of both women and men; they challenge us to perceive both feminine and masculine metaphors for God's presence in the world.

PRAYING WISDOM PSALMS

Some wisdom psalms for prayer include Psalms 1, 37, 49, 73, 112, 127, 128, 133, and 139. (Consult Appendix 1 for additional psalms of this type.) You might also focus on Torah Psalms, which praise God's teaching and law for peoples: Psalms 1, 19, 119. We begin, however, with three exercises to help us enter into the biblical wisdom tradition today.

PRAYING WITH YOUR EYES OPEN

Our lives are filled with ordinary tasks: eating a meal, washing the dishes, pulling weeds, dusting, washing your hands. But more attention-consuming tasks also fill our days: creating new products, caring for small children or elderly parents, completing a degree, paying bills, figuring taxes, running a household, teaching a classroom full of squirming children, clerking at a store, managing a small business, participating in volunteer organizations, ministering to a congregation, nursing the sick. Reflect on a typical day. What aspects of life become holy here? Is anyone present whom I usually overlook? How does the Spirit lead me in my everyday life?

THE VALIANT WOMAN

Another strand of the wisdom tradition describes the wise person (Prov 31:10–31). Describe a wise person— man, woman, or child—whom you know personally. What attributes of God does this person reflect to you?

LADY WISDOM

Still another strand of the wisdom tradition reflects on the gifts of God using feminine imagery. This can encourage us to broaden the images we use for God. The following two exercises invite us to experiment with various names and metaphors for God from the psalms.

1. Reflect on the following names and attributes for God taken from the rich variety in the psalms. How do both the names themselves and the juxtaposition of names and attributes affect your understanding of God? Your relationship to God?

God, Most High, you who are God of gods, over all other gods, unlike any other...

God, Creator, you who wear light as a robe, stretch out the heavens like a tent, build a palace above the waters, ride on the wings of the wind, appoint the wind as messenger...

God, Judge, you who judge the peoples with equity and truth, render to the proud their just deserts, are indignant every day because of injustice...

God, Holy One, you who dwell in a holy habitation, look down from a holy height, deal with us by your holy arm, lead us in your holy way, and offer us your holy promises...

God, King, strong and mighty, you who come in glory, sit enthroned above the flood, rule over all the earth, reign in the City of Zion, work salvation on the earth, love and execute justice, tend even the sparrow and swallow...

God, Father, you who lift up the poor from the dust, give the barren woman and orphan a home, and have compassion for all your children...

God, Mother, you comfort us as if we are a child on your lap, keep us safe upon your breast, and form us in the womb and birth us...

God, you who offer the shadow of your wings for refuge...

God, you who are like a fortress, a rock, a shield, water, light...

2. Create your own personal and intimate titles and attributes for God, addressing God directly within the context of your favorite psalm. For example, Nan Merrill (1998) prays Psalm 104: "Bless the Radiant One, O my soul! O Heart of my heart, You are so very great!"

KNOWING WHOSE I AM

Psalm 139 forms the basis of this guided meditation. If you are praying in a group, the psalm may be read by one voice and the reflection by another voice.

O LORD, you have searched me and known me.
You know when I sit down and when I rise up;
    you discern my thoughts from far away.
You search out my path and my lying down,
    and are acquainted with all my ways.

You are known, intimately....Ask yourself: How does it feel to be totally known? A relief? Frightening? Exciting?...Do you want to move toward the Knower? Or find some safety in which to hide?...Does it matter to you who it is who knows you?...

You hem me in, behind and before,
    and lay your hand upon me.

The experience of being known is like a fence, but is it a fence that provides security or keeps you bound? Or is it, paradoxically, both?

Such knowledge is too wonderful for me;
    it is so high that I cannot attain it.

Rest for some minutes in this paradox...

Where can I go from your spirit?
    Or where can I flee from your presence?
If I ascend to heaven, you are there;
    if I make my bed in Sheol, you are there.
If I take the wings of the morning
    and settle at the farthest limits of the sea,
even there your hand shall lead me,
    and your right hand shall hold me fast.
If I say, "Surely the darkness shall cover me,

and the light around me become night,"
even the darkness is not dark to you;
    the night is as bright as the day,
    for darkness is as light to you.

*Let the freedom that can come from being totally
known by a loving, merciful God seep gradually into
your being....Nothing to hide, no need for pretense, no
need to be anything other than exactly who you are....*

For it was you who formed my inward parts;
    you knit me together in my mother's womb.
I praise you, for I am fearfully and wonderfully made.
    Wonderful are your works;
that I know very well.
    My frame was not hidden from you,
when I was being made in secret,
    intricately woven in the depths of the earth.
Your eyes beheld my unformed substance.
In your book were written
    all the days that were formed for me,
    when none of them yet existed.

*Reflect on the deep connection between the creator and
the created, which we know best in the analogy of a
mother's love for her child...knowing that God's love
for you far surpasses the human situation.*

How weighty to me are your thoughts, O God!
    How vast is the sum of them!
I try to count them—they are more than the sand;
    I come to the end—I am still with you.

*Let the psalmist's wonder grow in you too....But, there
are violent parts to us; these too are known.*

O that you would kill the wicked, O God,
    and that the bloodthirsty would depart from me—
those who speak of you maliciously,

and lift themselves up against you for evil!
Do I not hate those who hate you, O LORD?
    And do I not loathe those who rise up against you?
I hate them with perfect hatred;
    I count them as my enemies.

*Can you bring even these parts of yourself to
God?...Can you admit to yourself what God already
knows?...Can you allow God to work in you at our
points of greatest weakness?...Can you let God work
any justice that is necessary?*

Search me, O God, and know my heart;
    test me and know my thoughts.
See if there is any wicked way in me,
    and lead me in the way everlasting.

Amen.... So be it....

LECTIO DIVINA ON WISDOM TEXTS

Lectio divina has appeared again and again in these
suggestions for praying the psalms. But perhaps there is
nothing more fitting for this form of prayer than the wisdom psalms. In this case the adage "form follows function" is certainly true. *Lectio divina* invites us to return to
the text over and over again, letting it settle daily in our
hearts. Wisdom psalms and the wisdom tradition remind
us that our call to holiness is a daily one, its expression
within the very ordinary actions of our lives.

• Select a helpful translation of Psalm 37, or another wisdom psalm to which you feel drawn.
• Allow the movements of *lectio divina* to flow in and out
of each other for as long as they are lively, or for the length
of time that you have set aside for prayer.
• At the conclusion of the *lectio divina* period, note in
your journal what happened; for example, the word or

phrase(s) you focused on, some of the ruminations or insights that came to you, the core of your response of God, and the "tone" of the contemplative moment.

You may wish to return to the same psalm at a second prayer time, allowing the repetition to carry you deeper in the same direction or into a new place in the same psalm. Journal as above. Repeat as long as the psalm still contains "energy" or until you feel finished.

> ## HANDMADE MIDRASH AND WRITING YOUR OWN PSALM

• Reflect on your daily life, either at home or at work. Create your own psalm after reflecting on your daily experience. You can repeat the phrase from Psalm 103:22 to provide a structure: "Bless the LORD, O my soul! for _____" *(complete with persons, objects, or actions)*. Now, select small items that you might use to create a visual representation of your everyday experience, such as paper clips, Post-Its, letterhead stationery, small screws or nails, seeds or clippings from garden catalogues, labels from food containers, cotton swabs or bandages— let your creative eye guide you to items representing places, actions, people, or things. Use these items to illustrate your "everyday" psalm.

• Discuss your creation with one other person. Ask the person what he or she sees in what you have done. Write in your journal, using some or all of the suggested questions in chapter 2. In particular, you may wish to notice the balance of feeling, form, and concept. What whole emerges through the parts?

• Reflect: What does creating your own "everyday psalm" deepen in you?

SINGING THE WISDOM PSALMS

• Select a wisdom psalm known to you and sing it several times, until it has impressed itself upon you. Try to memorize a portion of the psalm in this musical setting and sing it (interiorly or aloud) throughout the day. If your hymnal does not contain a setting for a wisdom psalm, take the verse above—"Bless the LORD, O my soul"—and create your own simple melody. Sing it frequently (aloud or to yourself) throughout the day.

Psalm	Title	Tune/Composer	Hymnal
1	Happy Are They	Haas	G
19	The Stars Declare His Glory	Deerfield	G
19	*Cantemos Al Señor*	Rosas	UMH, G, WOV
36	Come, O Font of Every Blessing	Nettleton	NCH
36	Immortal, Invisible, God Only Wise	St. Denio	NCH, W, G
73	Lord, Thee I Love with All My Heart	Herzlich Lieb DM	LBW
119	Happy Are They	Inwood	G&P
128	We Praise You	Ducote/Daigle	G&P
128	How Happy Is Each Child of God	Winchester Old	PH
133	How Pleasant	Jeong	NCH
133	Behold the Goodness of Our Lord	Cumond CM	PH
139	Lord Thou Hast Searched Me	Tender Thought	HEC
139	Wondrous Are Your Ways, Lord	Wennerberg	LBW

CORPORATE PSALM PRAYER: MORNING PRAYER

● Pray, with a group if possible, the following Morning Prayer. You may wish to sing the psalms for which music is available. This prayer should be adapted to your community, using its hymns, psalm hymns, and antiphons. The opening sentences, psalm prayers, and dismissal are adapted from *Daily Prayer* 1987, 70, 240, 251, 86.

Opening Sentences:
O Lord, open my lips. **And my mouth shall proclaim your praise.**
O depth of wealth, wisdom, and knowledge of God! **How unsearchable are God's judgments, how untraceable are God's ways!**
Source, Guide and Goal of all that is, **to God be glory forever! Amen.** (Rom 11:33, 36)

Morning Song: "Now Wisdom's Feast Continues"
(words by Elizabeth J. Smith; tune by Ellacombe)

Now Wisdom's feast continues, her well-aged wine
    still flows,
the bread of heaven fills us, and love of learning
    grows.
When faithful people listen, when hopeful people
    pray,
when loving people flourish, they show us Wisdom's
    way.

Through books and prayers and silence, in company,
    alone;
O Holy Wisdom, feed us and form us for your own.
And give us joy in learning, and help us in our turn
to hand on what you give us, that others, too, may
    learn.

For you are God our Teacher and drinking in your
  Word,
·we take to heart true wisdom and your whole church
  is stirred
to show the world your kindness, to teach the world
  your grace,
to bring the world, rejoicing, to greet you face to
  face.

Morning Song (alternative): Read Gerard Manley Hopkins's
poem "Pied Beauty."

Psalm 112 (sung antiphonally or in a hymn version)

Psalm Prayer
  Lord God, you have revealed your kindness to all
  people. Gather all nations to yourself, that in all the
  various tongues of the earth one hymn of praise may
  rise to you; through Jesus Christ our Lord. **Amen.**

Psalm 128 (alternately, Psalm 104)

Psalm Prayer
  God most high, by your Word you created a wondrous universe, and through your Spirit you breathed
  into it your breath of life. Accept creation's hymn of
  praise from our lips, and let the praise that is sung in
  heaven resound in the heart of every creature on
  earth, to your glory, Father, Son, and Holy Spirit,
  now and forever. **Amen.**

Reading: Proverbs 8 (especially vv. 22–31) or Wisdom of
Solomon 7:22—8:1

Silence

Gospel Canticle: Canticle of Zechariah (sung or recited
antiphonally)

Intercessions (or spontaneous prayers)

The Lord's Prayer

Concluding Sentences
> To God be honor and glory forever! **Amen.** (1 Tim 1:17)
> Bless the Lord. **The Lord's name be praised.**

Psalm 112

1   Praise the LORD!
      Happy are those who fear the LORD,
      who greatly delight in his commandments.

2   Their descendants will be mighty in the land;
      the generation of the upright will be blessed.

3   Wealth and riches are in their houses,
      and their righteousness endures forever.

4   They rise in the darkness as a light for the
        upright;
      they are gracious, merciful, and righteous.

5   It is well with those who deal generously and lend,
      who conduct their affairs with justice.

6   For the righteous will never be moved;
      they will be remembered forever.

7   They are not afraid of evil tidings;
      their hearts are firm, secure in the LORD.

8   Their hearts are steady, they will not be afraid;
      in the end they will look in triumph on their
        foes.

9   They have distributed freely, they have given to
        the poor;
      their righteousness endures forever;
      their horn is exalted in honor.

10   The wicked see it and are angry;
      they gnash their teeth and melt away;
      the desire of the wicked comes to nothing.

Nine

Knowing Ourselves Through the Psalms: Psalms as Mirror of Our Lives

Our approach to psalms has focused on human experiences, such as joy and suffering, longing and gratitude. We have searched for a commonality between the life experience of Israel's singers and people of our own era, hoping to learn anew some long-tested ways of praying in groups and in private. Lamenting, praising, and thanking are all common human and religious experiences that bridge the ancient and modern worlds, so when we speak of psalms from this perspective, we might describe the interpretive approach as human-centered or anthropological.

In this chapter we listen to readings of psalms that touch our spiritual and religious experience because we can imagine similar feelings and emotions and language in our own lives or the lives of those around us. We begin with personal and contemporary experience by which a psalm helps us better to interpret our own spiritual lives, and then revisit some great spiritual teachers of the past,

189

notably John Calvin (sixteenth century) and Athanasius (fourth century). We conclude with a powerful reflection on Psalm 23 viewed through the prism of a person who experienced sexual abuse during childhood.

A PERSONAL EXPERIENCE OF HEZEKIAH'S PRAYER

A psalm embedded in Isaiah 38 helped me (John) to understand important aspects of my relationships and spirituality. A friend and I had taught on the same faculty for several years and had team-taught a course one year. At the time, I was experiencing serious disruption from an illness that was later diagnosed as chronic fatigue syndrome, and on several occasions my colleague attempted to console and help me. In confidence, my friend revealed his HIV status to me. Later he moved to another city, and we had only occasional communication. Several years later I heard from others that he now suffered from AIDS. As he neared death, I flew to the city where he was then living to visit him. On the plane I thought of Hezekiah's prayer in Isaiah 38, the one that begins: "In the noontide of my days I must depart." This text touched me deeply, for I was going to visit a man about to die "at the noontide of his life."

During the visit, we decided to pray together, and I mentioned this text. I read it slowly, and we paused to speak about my friend's experiences, mirrored in the agonizing words attributed to King Hezekiah, and we prayed to God for his comforting. I was acutely aware of the ending of this prayer—an exuberant thanksgiving to God for a healing—which was not to be my friend's experience. Since that time I have always paused, often with sorrow, every time I hear that particular text and remember my friend. I pray for him and others I've known who have died "in the noontide" of their lives.

This psalm continues to act like a mirror for me, regularly pushing an important part of my past life into consciousness, reminding me of the stark reality of early death, of the sadness over dashed hopes and expectations, of the loss my friend's death occasioned—all significant parts of human experience remembered in prayer.

Only in retrospect, and rather recently, have I begun to "hear" this psalm also in connection with my experience of chronic fatigue syndrome and to give great thanks to God for the care and healing I have experienced. When recounting this story during a retreat with psalms, I realized that I could also pray the latter part of the prayer (vv. 17–20) in thanksgiving for my own healing. Not only does the psalm remind me of past events, but the movement from grief to joy helps me grasp part of my own experience in a new and prayerful way.

KATHLEEN NORRIS ON THE PSALMS

Contemporary writer Kathleen Norris recounts stories by women who find their experience reflected in regular praying of psalms. In *The Cloister Walk* she writes fondly of two lengthy sabbaticals she spent in the Benedictine atmosphere of St. John's Abbey in Collegeville, Minnesota. She was fascinated by the monasticism she experienced there, especially the regular pattern of the Liturgy of the Hours. As a Protestant observing the Benedictine tradition, she writes not with critical eyes but with a sense of wonder and affection.

The pages of her journal bubble over with sage and wry comments on daily life and daily prayer with the psalms. One chapter, entitled "The Paradox of the Psalms," shows how the psalms can help us to see ourselves more clearly, honestly, and lovingly. After growing up thinking that she had to look and be her best to go into church, she had a new experience with the Liturgy of the Hours.

> I learned that when you go to church several times a day, every day, there is no way you can "do it right." You are not always going to sit up straight, let alone think holy thoughts. You're not going to wear your best clothes but whatever isn't in the dirty clothes basket. You come to the Bible's great "book of praises" through all the moods and conditions of life, and while you may feel like hell, you sing anyway. To your surprise, you find that the psalms do not deny your true feelings but allow you to reflect on them, right in front of God and everyone. I soon realized, during my first residency at St. John's, that this is not easy to do on a daily basis. (Norris 1996, 92)

Later she describes the ordinary and mundane experience of learning what life is really like from her growing acquaintance with the psalms and with the nuns.

> One sister told me that when she first entered the convent as an idealistic young woman, she had tried to pretend that "praise was enough." It didn't last long. The earthy honesty of the psalms had helped her, she says, to "get real, get past the holy talk and the romantic image of the nun." In expressing all the complexities and contradictions of human experience, the psalms act as good psychologists. They defeat our tendency to try to be holy without being human first. Psalm 6 mirrors the way in which our grief and anger are inextricably mixed; the lament that "I am exhausted with my groaning; every night

I drench my pillow with tears" (v. 6) soon leads to rage: "I have grown old surrounded by my foes. Leave me, you who do evil" (vv. 7–8). Psalm 38 stands on the precipice of depression, as wave after wave of bitter self-accusation crashes against the small voice of hope. The psalm is clinically accurate in its portrayal of extreme melancholia: "the very light has gone from my eyes" (v. 10), "my pain is always before me" (v. 17), and its praise is found only in the possibility of hope: "It is for you, O Lord, that I wait" (v. 15). The psalms make us uncomfortable because they don't allow us to deny either the depth of our pain or the possibility of its transformation into praise. (Norris 1996, 96)

She also noticed how psalms that we know very well help us to interpret for ourselves some of life's most difficult and challenging moments.

But what often happens is that holiness reasserts itself so that even familiar psalms suddenly infuse the events of one's life with new meaning. One sister told me that as she prayed the psalms aloud at the bedside of her dying mother, who was in a coma, she discovered "how perfectly the psalms reflected my own inner chaos: my fear of losing her, or of not losing her and seeing her suffer more, of saying goodbye, of being motherless." She found that the closing lines of Psalm 16—"You will show me the path of life, the fullness of joy in your presence"—consoled her, "as I saw my mother slipping away. I was able to turn her life over to God." (Norris 1996, 100)

Kathleen Norris's attentive listening to these women prayers of the psalms shows how they grew in self-awareness and spirituality as they found their inner lives and experiences reflected in the words and phrases from many, many centuries ago. In this sense we can also speak of the psalms as the anatomy of the human soul. In a similar vein, Eugene Peterson remarks of the psalms: They "are necessary because they are the prayer masters....We apprentice ourselves to these masters, acquiring facility in using the tools, by which we become more and more ourselves" (Peterson 1989, 3–4). In a very real sense the psalms usher us into a rich world of shared human experience, a world wherein we can locate ourselves. The psalms deliver us from the need to analyze and to define every event, described by Norris as "the tyranny of individual experience" (Norris 1996, 100). Even more important, in an age concerned with the experiential bases of spirituality and theology, the wealth of human experience lodged within the psalms reminds us not to consider our individual experiences as deep or broad enough to fashion our vision of the world. We shall now turn to other spiritual writers on the psalms who saw this link between life experience and the world of the psalms.

ATHANASIUS OF ALEXANDRIA

Athanasius of Alexandria, the fourth-century bishop and theologian, made this point in his letter to Marcellinus on the interpretation of the Psalms:

> For in addition to the other things in which it enjoys an affinity and fellowship with the other books, it possesses, beyond that, this marvel of its own— namely, that it contains even the emotions of each soul, and it has the changes and rectifications of these delineated and regulated in itself. Therefore anyone who wishes boundlessly to receive and

> understand from it, so as to mold himself, it is writ-
> ten there. (Athanasius 1980, 108)

He describes the way in which the words of the psalms,
unlike other biblical texts, can become our own words:
"And the one who hears is deeply moved, as though he
himself were speaking, and is affected by the words of the
songs as if they were his own songs" (Athanasius 1980,
#11, 109). The person praying them need not hesitate to
pray the very words of the texts, for

> he who recites the Psalms is uttering the rest as his
> own words, and each sings them as if they were writ-
> ten concerning him, and he accepts them and recites
> them not as if another were speaking, nor as if speak-
> ing about someone else. But he handles them as if he
> is speaking about himself. And the things spoken are
> such that he lifts them up to God as himself acting
> and speaking them from himself....[Whoever] chants
> these will be especially confident in speaking what is
> written as if his own and about him. (Athanasius
> 1980, #11, 110)

In sum, the psalms reveal our true selves to us as well as
to others: "For the Psalms comprehend the one who
observes the commandment as well as the one who trans-
gresses, and the action of each" (Athanasius 1980, #11,
110). For Athanasius, the psalms can teach us, because
they contain the breadth of prayer of the human spirit: "If
the point needs to be put more forcefully, let us say that
the entire Holy Scripture is a teacher of virtues and of the
truths of faith, while the Book of Psalms possesses somehow the perfect image for the souls' course of life"
(Athanasius 1980, #14, 112).

AMBROSE OF MILAN

In the same century a Western writer used a different image to utter something very similar about the psalms. Ambrose of Milan, legendary originator of Christian hymnody and teacher of Augustine, commented:

> Though all of Scripture is fragrant with God's grace, the Book of Psalms has a special attractiveness....All who read it may find the cure for their own individual failings. All with eyes to see can discover in it a complete gymnasium for the soul, a stadium for all the virtues, equipped for every kind of exercise; it is for each to choose the kind he judges best to help him gain the prize. (Ambrose 1975, 543f.)

His metaphor, the gymnasium of the soul, suggests the similarity of regular exercise for the body and a similar pattern of prayer for the soul.

MARTIN LUTHER

In *Preface to the Psalms* Martin Luther spoke of the psalms as authentic witness to the lives of the saints, because it proposed the deepest yearnings and prayers of their hearts and is far more important than their deeds. Contrary to many of his other writings on the psalms, where he sees many psalms as prophecies of Christ, he speaks here of psalms fit for every human need and concern:

> For every man on every occasion can find in it Psalms which fit his needs, which he feels to be as

appropriate as if they had been set there just for his sake....And there follows from this a further excellence that when some such a word has come home and is felt to answer his need, he receives assurance that he is in the company of the saints. (Dillenberger 1961, 40)

JOHN CALVIN

John Calvin (1509–64) taught that study of the psalms can lead to a deep, interior knowledge of the human person through careful attention to David's psychology. For this reason they provide a guide to prayer, especially to praise of God and also complaints to God. In *The Author's Preface to the Commentary on the Book of Psalms* Calvin provides a retrospective look at his own life and work:

> I have been accustomed to call this book, I think not inappropriately, "An Anatomy of all the Parts of the Soul"; for there is not an emotion of which anyone can be conscious that is not here represented as in a mirror. Or rather, the Holy Spirit has here drawn to the life all the griefs, sorrows, fears, doubts, hopes, cares, perplexities, in short, all the distracting emotions with which the minds of people are wont to be agitated. (Dillenberger 1975, 23)

Calvin is as convinced as others that psalms provide a model for our prayer:

> Calling upon God is one of the principal means of assuring our safety, and as a better and more unerring rule for guiding us in this exercise cannot be

found elsewhere than in The Psalms; genuine and
earnest prayer proceeds first from a sense of our
need, and next, from faith in the promises of God. It
is by perusing these inspired compositions, that men
will be most effectually awakened to a sense of their
maladies, and at the same time, instructed in seeking
remedies for their cure. In short, whatever may serve
to encourage us when we are about to pray to God,
is taught us in this book. (Dillenberger 1975, 23)

But the most compelling reason for Calvin to pray the
psalms derives from his personal identification with
David, their traditional author. Calvin could find in
David's experience a mirror for the tribulations of his
own life, so he pondered the psalms of David while struggling with the responsibilities of his own ministry. After
mentioning various conflicts and trials of his own life, he
continues:

in considering the whole course of the life of David,
it seemed to me that by his own footsteps he showed
me the way, and from this I have experienced no
small consolation....I have been assailed on all sides,
and have scarcely been able to enjoy repose for a single moment, but have always had to sustain some
conflict either from enemies without or within the
church....But since the condition of David was such,
that though he had deserved well of his own people,
he was nevertheless bitterly hated by many without a
cause...it afforded me no small consolation...to con-
form myself to the example of so great and so excellent a person....In my meditations upon [the Psalms]
I did not wander, as it were, in an unknown region.
(Dillenberger 1975, 28–32)

In these reflections Calvin's approach to the psalms is human
centered, focusing on their appropriation and revelation

of the human psyche and soul. These qualities allow the psalms to teach us how to pray.

PAUL VI

The tradition of using psalmody during the times of daily prayer that comprise the Liturgy of the Hours also allows for a human-oriented way of praying psalms. Pope Paul VI's introduction to the Liturgy of the Hours discusses the psalms, especially as they reflect human circumstances:

> Each psalm was written in its own individual circumstances....Each psalm has its own meaning, which we cannot overlook even in our own day. Though the psalms originated very many centuries ago in the East they express accurately the pain and hope, the unhappiness and trust, of people of every age and country, and celebrate especially faith in God, revelation and redemption. (Paul VI 1975, #107)

When people pray the psalms, they should attend to the genuine human emotions and yearnings found in these ancient prayers. Paul VI continues, "In keeping to the meaning of the words the person who prays the psalms is looking for the human value of the text for the life of faith" (#107). Although the instruction also explains how Christians pray the psalms in the person of the church and of Christ, the human values and aspirations of the psalms stand out as extremely significant for Christian prayer "for people of every age and country."

PSALM 23: SHEPHERDING THE MOURNERS

Psalm 23 is a powerful example of a text that draws human experience back to consciousness. In the United States the "Shepherd Psalm" has become the most popular of all, especially for use at funerals and memorial services (Holladay 1993, 359–69). Many people—including those who are not churchgoers—choose it in times of sorrow both because of the consoling images of a shepherd caring for survivors and because of the trust that this shepherd-like Lord will provide a table and eternal rest for the deceased. Frequently those who hear Psalm 23 are reminded of a loved one's funeral, drawn to recollection of that person's life, their relationship with that person, the sadness and joys, the loss, and the gratitude for the life of the deceased. One might affirm the comment of Calvin that in the psalms "the Holy Spirit has here drawn to life all the griefs, sorrows, fears, doubts, hopes, cares, per-plexities…with which the minds of people are wont to be agitated" (Dillenberger 1975, 23).

PSALM 23 FOR SURVIVORS OF ABUSE

We can hear Psalm 23 outside of funerals. Pastoral the-ologian Nancy Ramsay has pondered this psalm in her roles as teacher and pastoral counselor, where she often deals with survivors of childhood sexual abuse. But she has also "heard" the psalm in a much more personal light, for she writes "as a survivor of incest perpetrated by a member of my extended family."

Ramsay chose Psalm 23 because "it reflects the trust of one who has experienced severe trauma that threatened death" and because its primary concern is the "trustworthy and empowering compassion of God" (Ramsay 1998, 220). She describes the effects of such abuse as "radical suffering." Such suffering differs from the normal suffering that most people expect and undergo in three ways: It is completely undeserved, it is totally unanticipated, and it results from intentional violation and harm at the hands of another. Survivors of radical suffering cannot accept traditional interpretations of suffering as either instructive or character building, or as deserved because of their own actions or behavior. This kind of suffering defiles the image of God in the victim, because child sexual abuse makes people into bearers of shame, a condition that utterly robs them of a sense of value, of being created good and in God's image (Gen 1:27–28). To destroy the image of God in a human being ultimately leads to defiling the vision of God's love and power. The victim finds it difficult to experience God as a shepherd who exercises power in a trustworthy manner.

A central aspect of Ramsay's reflections on this psalm concerns the well-known verse "Surely goodness and mercy shall follow me all the days of my life, and I shall dwell in the house of the Lord for ever" (v. 6, RSV). In common parlance, "goodness and mercy" radiate gentle, soft, and cozy feelings, which may account for part of the psalm's appeal. But "goodness" in this verse derives from the same word that reports God's assessment and aesthetic of creation in Genesis 1, "And God saw that it was good." It refers here to the way in which creation beautifully fulfills God's purposes and intentions for it, which includes relationships of justice that guard and preserve shalom.

The Hebrew word translated "love" is *hesed*, often translated as "steadfast love" and considered a description of the binding and preserving love between God and all those included in the covenant with God. Finally the word "follows" might much more accurately be rendered as "pursues." The psalmist declares that God's creative vision and covenantal care shall literally pursue this singer all the days of his or her life.

Such a notion of God's passionate concern for creation, for humans, and especially for vulnerable humans comes to center stage in Ramsay's reflections on this psalm. A long process of study and self-reflection led her to a new way of perceiving God: "I have come to imagine God's love as fierce tenderness" (Ramsay 1998, 219). For her, this image combines the love and justice of God, focuses on God's concern for the vulnerable and oppressed, and shows God's compassion as "trustworthy and empowering," which stands as the exact opposite of the abusive use of power by predators. God as shepherd exercises fierce advocacy on behalf of the weak and wounded, just "the sort of fierce tenderness parents afford their vulnerable young" (Ramsay 1998, 220). The rod and the staff in verse 4 represent God's ongoing action for protection and liberation from fear and shame for the victim of abuse; while acknowledging the ongoing existence of such evil and its effects, it affirms God's designs for a very different reality. In subtle ways Ramsay rereads Psalm 23 to affirm God's compassion as a fierce tenderness, a power directed toward protection and liberation of the abused (Ramsay 1998, 219–20).

After offering her listeners a new image of God, Ramsay develops a goal of pastoral care for survivors of abuse: How can we incarnate such love in ways that counter the fear and shame they experience? Pastoral caregivers must recognize the fierce and protective compassion of God for the victims to whom they minister, but they need to demonstrate it by ministering in ways that demonstrate compassion and are empowering and completely trustworthy. Such a lifestyle incarnates God's love in our lives. Her reading of verse 5 offers explicit suggestions for pastoral care in an ecclesial setting: "You prepare a table before me in the presence of my enemies; you anoint my head with oil; my cup overflows." Reflecting on God's setting a table and anointing with oil can suggest "the power of ritual to make the vision of God's fierce tenderness real to survivors" (Ramsay 1998, 224). Particularly appropriate expressions of the table setting can be experienced in celebration of the Lord's Supper, while "the image of oil also suggests the empowering possibilities of services of healing and wholeness which offer anointing with oil that symbolizes God's blessing" (ibid.).

We, her listeners, may suspect that in suggesting these core Christian rituals as agents of God's love and compassionate desire to heal, we hear reflected some of her own spiritual experience of God's fierce tenderness in her life. One does not need to know or to pray Psalm 23 in order to recognize the horror of the shame and suffering experienced by survivors of childhood sexual abuse, but her reading of it surely deepens her self-awareness as a daughter of God, created in God's image, rightfully claiming the fierce protection of the God who created her and invited her to covenant. Meditation, reflection, and prayer on this psalm actually mirror different aspects of her life, as a survivor herself, as a pastoral caregiver "incarnating" such love in concrete ways, and as a teacher helping others to discover the implications of childhood sexual abuse for theology, spirituality, and ministry. For her, and for many survivors, this psalm can offer an authentic path to much deeper knowledge of herself, her radical suffering, and God's compassion that should be mediated in the church.

Should we use the psalms as our mirror? Long and constant tradition says "yes!" From such psalms as Psalm 23 we absorb the idiom and attitude of the psalms, an attitude of familiarity with God, boldness in address to God, comprehensiveness, honesty, and empathy. Then, perhaps even without our adverting to it directly, the figure and ground reverse. Instead of praying the psalms, the psalms pray us.

PRAYING THE PSALMS, THE PSALMS PRAYING US

This chapter focused not on a particular genre of psalms but on the dynamic creativity that they work in the heart of the one who prays them deeply. The psalms you select for prayer will be very much your own choice. Nonetheless, some mirrorlike psalms include Psalms 4, 6, 16, 17, 18, 22, 26, 38, 40, 42, 43, 51, 62, 63, 69, 71, 101, 102, 116, 130, 131, and 139. Psalms can also mirror our community's life, whether family, church, or nation. Here you may pray over Psalms 2, 10, 12, 33, 44, 46, 47, 53, 67, 68, 74, 78, 79, 80, 85, 105, 106, 107, 126, 127, 133, and 137.

PERSONAL IDENTITY DISCOVERED IN PSALMS

• Placing yourself in God's presence, examine favorite psalms for what you learn about yourself. Ask the Holy Spirit to reveal how this psalm might reflect your own life's movements. This learning may come from the text of the psalm directly or from the response that the psalm stirs up in you, such as delight, anger, resistance, yearning. On one day a psalm may welcome you, on another day the same psalm may carry a note of judgment. Speak about the "you" reflected there directly to God.

PERSONAL IDENTITY EXPRESSED
THROUGH PSALMS

• Search for a psalm that expresses who you are before God at this moment in your life. Repeat appropriate verses in the style of *lectio divina* as a kind of prayer of your heart to God.

HANDMADE MIDRASH

• Comb the psalms for phrases that express something important about who you are before God. Then render these phrases into a visual self-portrait, with or without using the written text. You might choose to do a word collage, a collage constructed of the images evoked by the self-descriptive phrases, or a combination. Discuss your self-portrait with one other person. How does your self-portrait correspond with your inner thoughts and feelings? See chapter 2 for other questions.
• Write in your journal, using some or all of the suggestions in chapter 2. What is the most important thing that happened to you as you created this midrash?
• Offer yourself to God in whatever way seems appropriate.

WRITE YOUR OWN PSALM

• Choosing one of the communities to which you belong, write a psalm that expresses your community's situation, needs, struggles, and desires to God. What do you want God to do for your community? Who do you want God to be for your community?

EXPRESSING A PSALM IN MOVEMENT

• After praying on the text of Psalm 139, tape record yourself speaking the words of the psalm slowly. Replay the tape as many times as you like, allowing aspects of the psalm to come alive in movement. For example, you may wish to enact yourself being knitted together in your mother's womb. Reflect on how this activity has deepened your understanding of yourself.

SINGING THE PSALMS

Psalm	Title	Tune/Composer	Hymnal
63	O God, You Are My God	St. Bride SM	PH
63	Psalm 63: As Morning Breaks	Joncas	G
63	I Long for You	Balhoff/Daigle/Ducote	G, G&P
63	I Will Lift up My Eyes	Conry	G, G&P
63	God Is My Great Desire	Leoni	W
63	I Will Bless God	Peña	NCH
139	You Are Before Me, Lord	Sursum Corda (Smith)	PH
139	Filling Me with Joy	Lesicky	G
139	Lord, Thou Hast Searched Me	Tender Thought	HEC
139	Wondrous Are Your Ways	Wennerberg	LBW
139	You Are Near	Schutte	G&P
139	Search Me, O God	Marshall	NCH

COMMUNAL EVENING PRAYER

• Pray the following Evening Prayer in common, if possible. Use your community's hymnal to select appropriate hymns, antiphons, and psalms for singing.

Service of Light

> Light and peace in Jesus Christ our Lord. **Thanks be to God.**
>
> *Hymn:* "Phos Hilaron" or another suitable evening hymn

Psalm 86

Psalm Prayer

> O God, you hear the movements of our hearts and you come to our assistance. For even when we do not know how to pray, your Spirit intercedes for us with sighs too deep for words. May we trust that in your mercy and love you will shed light upon our heart's desires so that we may come to know ourselves in you and you in us. We pray this in the name of Jesus and in the power of his Spirit. **Amen.**

Psalm 119:145–52

Psalm Prayer

> Gracious God, you call us to walk in the light of Christ. Free us from darkness and keep us in the radiance of your truth. We ask this through Christ, your Son, who lives and reigns with you and the Holy Spirit, one God, forever and ever. **Amen.**

Reading: 2 Corinthians 4:6–11

Silence

Gospel Canticle: Canticle of Mary (sung or recited antiphonally)

Intercessory Prayers: To all prayers, respond: **Hear us, O Lord.**

We bring the prayers of our hearts and minds before you God, recognizing your presence among all peoples. We rely on your healing power and your desire for justice in our world.
Let us pray for the church...
Let us pray for the world...
Let us pray for those in need...
Let us pray for the sick and dying...
Let us pray for ourselves...

The Lord's Prayer

Concluding Prayer

Gracious God, yours is the morning and yours is the evening. Let the Sun of Justice, Jesus Christ, shine forever in our hearts and draw us to that light where you live in radiant glory. We ask this in the name of Jesus our friend, through the life of the Holy Spirit. **Amen.**

May the Lord bless us, protect us from all evil, and bring us to everlasting life. **Amen.**

Psalm 24

1   The earth is the LORD's and all that is in it,
    the world, and those who live in it;
2   for he has founded it on the seas,
    and established it on the rivers.
3   Who shall ascend the hill of the LORD?
    And who shall stand in his holy place?
4   Those who have clean hands and pure hearts,
    who do not lift up their souls to what is false,
    and do not swear deceitfully.
5   They will receive blessing from the LORD,
    and vindication from the God of their
      salvation.
6   Such is the company of those who seek him,
    who seek the face of the God of Jacob. *Selah*

7   Lift up your heads, O gates!
    and be lifted up, O ancient doors!
    that the King of glory may come in.
8   Who is the King of glory?
    The LORD, strong and mighty,
    the LORD, mighty in battle.
9   Lift up your heads, O gates!
    and be lifted up, O ancient doors!
    that the King of glory may come in.
10   Who is this King of glory?
    The LORD of hosts,
    he is the King of glory. *Selah*

Ten

Praying Psalms in, with, and through Jesus Christ: Christological Psalms

Often we reflect on our own feelings and hopes and situations through the example of a revered person or an important leader. Faith-filled people regularly repeat prayers of their ancestors in the faith, of those considered holy in their traditions. Roman Catholics have a long tradition of repeating prayers of favorite saints. For Luther, the psalms represent the prayer life of the saints. Some of his hymns derived from psalms illuminate his own prayer life and remain favorites to this day, especially "A Mighty Fortress is our God." Simkha Y. Weintraub remarks of Psalm 90: "It announces itself— quite uniquely—as 'A prayer of Moses, the man of God.' If Moses could say this, then surely we will benefit from his words" (Weintraub 1994, 73). For Christians, the prayer Jesus taught his disciples, the Lord's Prayer, has become the "great prayer."

For sheer number of prayers, however, David is the great hero and example because of the tradition that he composed the psalms. In chapter 5 we noticed how David became the premier example of one who prayed, so a great number of psalms were attributed to him in the superscriptions. One might pray Psalm 3 differently knowing it was "a psalm of David, when he fled from his son Absalom." Those who feel hunted by an enemy can pray Psalm 57, especially when they hear how Saul pursued David: "Of David. A Miktam, when he fled from Saul, in the cave." See also Psalms 54, 56, 59, 60, 142; in each a superscript title refers to an event in David's life. But one could pray with David's words not only in times of distress. Many psalms were clearly connected to happier events in his life, including Psalms 9, 18, 30, 34. So many psalms connect with David in their titles that religious people have long speculated on the events in his life that may have occasioned each psalm. As time passed, the Jewish people took comfort in David's examples of prayer, and they began to assign more and more psalms to him. When the psalms were translated into Greek, that version contained many more "Davidic" titles than the Hebrew Book of Psalms. Truly, David is a model of prayer, and countless numbers of Jews and Christians have drawn spiritual nurture not only from his prayers but also from imagining his praying of these psalms.

PSALMS AND JESUS CHRIST

Similarly, Christians have paid attention to both the words and the style of the prayer of Jesus. We may assume that Jesus, like other Jews of his time, grew up hearing and singing the psalms in daily prayer, on the Sabbath, and at the great pilgrimage festivals. Our information about psalms in first-century synagogues suggests that their regular use served two purposes: first, remembering the

Temple; and second, fulfilling the divine command to "love the LORD thy God" by daily praise (Werner 1960, 156). Each day of the week had certain psalms attached to it in ancient times, and this pattern may provide a glimpse back to the time of Jesus. They are mentioned along with other prayer suggestions later in this chapter.

The New Testament contains citations from thirty-six psalms, fifty-five citations in all (Holladay 1993, 115). In the synoptic gospels the psalm citations are fairly evenly divided between the accounts of Jesus' ministry and those of the passion narrative. Very few of these citations actually concern prayer; more often they become teaching sayings of Jesus or ways of interpreting events. The evangelists clearly understood Jesus' life and ministry in the deeply religious context of the Jewish scriptures, especially the psalms. We cannot always know with confidence whether Jesus actually cited or alluded to a psalm, or whether those who narrated the gospels "remembered" these events through the prism of constantly heard psalms. Much of the New Testament evidence suggests that we can understand Jesus better by knowing the psalms that inspired spiritual reflection on his life.

A PSALM FOR PALM SUNDAY AND EASTER: PSALM 118

Psalm 118 originated as a song of thanksgiving for victory in a battle that threatened Israel and its king. Early Christians heard in this psalm several important allusions to Jesus Christ, so it now serves as a focal psalm for Holy Week and the Easter season. We will explore verses of this psalm that feature prominently in Christian liturgy and hymnody.

As we encounter Psalm 118 on Palm Sunday, we can focus on two verses that crystallize much of what we celebrate this day.

> 25 Save us, we beseech you, O LORD!
> O LORD, we beseech you, give us success!
> 26 Blessed is the one who comes in the name of the LORD.
> We bless you from the house of the LORD.

In verse 25 the Hebrew for "save us, we beseech you" is *Hoshia-na,* which comes to us as "Hosanna." It is an imperative, a command addressed to God *(hoshia)* with a word added to mean something like "please" *(-na).* The Hosannas that Christians sing have become words of praise and exultation, while the Hebrew text may reverberate with a sense of the longing and yearning of the Jewish inhabitants of Jerusalem, caught up in an oppressive and disastrous Roman policy. "Save us, O LORD" may capture their shouts of hope for a leader who could deliver them, give them success and victory. Perhaps the very words of this verse capture some of the ambiguity of Jesus' entry into Jerusalem. In an unexpected way God did save and grant victory through Christ's dying and rising.

In verse 26 the crowds proclaim, "Blessed is the one who comes in the name of the LORD." Originally this "one who comes" referred to any devout Israelite who came to the festival celebration, but in later Judaism it became a messianic title, as when the disciples of John the Baptist asked Jesus, "Are you the *one who is to come,* or are we to wait for another?" (Matt 11:3). In Christian tradition it took on a decidedly christological sense, as we proclaim regularly at Eucharist: "Blessed is he who comes in the name of the Lord." The translation "blessed is the one"

214 • A RETREAT WITH THE PSALMS

picks up the earlier sense of the psalm. In contemporary English it conveys a more inclusive note, that all are welcome in the house of the Lord. Those who proclaim "Blessed is he who comes in the name of the Lord," however, may combine this notion of ancient worship and psalmody with the entry of Christ into Jerusalem on Palm Sunday and into our hearts anew each time we proclaim these words. Here we witness the difference between a christological hearing of a psalm (verse) and a human-oriented understanding of it.

When we hear or sing Psalm 118 on Easter Sunday, we normally focus on verses 22–24:

22 The stone that the builders rejected
    has become the chief cornerstone.
23 This is the LORD's doing;
    it is marvelous in our eyes.
24 This is the day that the LORD has made;
    let us rejoice and be glad in it.

We recognize the Easter antiphon in verse 24 from many beautiful ways of singing it during this season of joy. In verse 22 we meet a core metaphor for what has happened to Christ as God raised him from the dead. The image came to Christians through this psalm, into which this proverbial saying had been inserted. Imagine stonecutters selecting stone for an impressive building. One of the pieces seems such an odd shape that they toss it on a trash pile. Later, when looking for a capstone (a V-shaped stone to brace an arch at its central point) or a cornerstone, this bit of debris suddenly finds its place and function; it now anchors the entire structure. What a reversal—from garbage heap to linchpin, from dust to riches, from lament to praise! As a metaphor for reversal of fortunes, this saying introduces the plea for God's saving action in verse 25: "LORD, grant salvation!" Praying this psalm conscious of

Jesus crucified and risen, early Christians understood it as prophecy of Christ's resurrection. For Christians, this verse helps us to ponder the amazing reversal in Jesus' life, where death is "swallowed up in victory!"

AN ENTRANCE PSALM FOR THE LORD, THE ARK, AND JESUS: PSALM 24

Psalm 24 is often described as a liturgical psalm, reminiscent of entrance processions with the ark of the covenant into the Jerusalem Temple. Some rabbis considered it the psalm composed for the procession with the ark when Solomon dedicated the Temple; another Jewish commentator, David Kimchi, argued that David prepared it for the ceremony when he brought the ark into the city of Jerusalem (Sarna 1993, 129). The worshipers would have begun with a chorus praising the God of all creation:

1   The earth is the LORD'S and all that is in it,
     the world, and those who live in it;
2   for he has founded it on the seas,
     and established it on the rivers.

The song begins by praising God as creator and ruler over all the universe. When Paul explained to the Corinthians how all kinds of meat sold in the markets were permissible, for everything belongs to God, he cited verse 1: "For the earth and its fullness are the Lord's" (1 Cor 10:26). In verses 3–6, however, the psalm shifts, and some interpreters think that a second choir joined in here:

3   Who may go up the mountain of the LORD?
     Who can stand in his holy place? (RNAB)

These questions cause those in the procession to reflect on their own state of preparedness to enter into the holy precincts of the Temple: Have they followed the stipulations of the Torah, and are they ready to participate in worship? Verses 5 and 6 proclaim that those who are prepared shall receive great blessings from God when they seek the LORD in love and justice. So the first six verses combine a hymn of praise to God with a reminder about readiness to enter into worship.

The last three verses (vv. 7–10) shift to another scene: The worshipers and the ark have arrived at the gate of the Temple precincts. They all stop there and engage in a dialogue for entry into the sacred area. In Christian worship the "king of glory" who seeks to enter has become Jesus, the King of the Jews. These verses have been memorialized in song and music. One of the most popular is Willard Jabusch's "The King of Glory," often sung on Palm Sunday. The refrain and first verse of the hymn pick up questions and responses of Psalm 24:7–10; the rest of the verses of the hymn review Jesus' life and mission.

A well-known chorus from Handel's *Messiah* also brings these psalm verses to listeners, especially during Advent and at Easter: "Lift up your heads" (#33). Christians automatically connect these renditions of Psalm 24:7–10 with Jesus Christ, the king of glory who enters into the city of Jerusalem acclaimed by crowds on Palm Sunday. God's saving presence, originally symbolized in the Israelite ark, which even led them into battle and later resided in the Temple, has taken on a new meaning after the death and resurrection of Jesus. They are more likely to imagine God made flesh in Jesus Christ, who came to save humankind as the King of Glory about whom they sing. We should be pleased when this psalm is sung liturgically during Advent, for the Ascension (Reformed tradition), and for the Presentation of the Lord (Catholic); sung psalmody has helped to shape our memory and our spiritual appropriation of these events in Christ's life. Next we will look back to the New Testament and early Christian writers to see how extensive were these christological interpretations of Israel's psalms.

PSALMS AS PROPHETIC OF JESUS' PASSION AND DEATH

Early Christians read the Psalms of David as prophetic texts that pointed to events in their own time and especially in the life of Jesus Christ. Psalm 118 is an excellent example. This practice of prophetic interpretation of psalms is most clear in Luke and Acts. An excellent example appears in the Emmaus story, when Jesus walked with two of his disciples on the road on the day of his resurrection. Jesus explained to the two astonished disciples "all that the prophets have declared" (Luke 24:25). When they returned to Jerusalem and narrated their experience of the risen Jesus to their companions, Jesus appeared in the midst of their gathering and repeated his prophetic claim: "'These are my words that I spoke to you while I was still with you—that everything written about me in the law of Moses, the prophets and the *psalms* must be fulfilled.' Then he opened their minds to understand the scriptures" (Luke 24:44–45, emphasis added). For these early Christians the value of the psalms was that they spoke prophetically. For them, the psalms did not function so much as prayers, but as oracles that proclaimed who Jesus was.

Early Christians were not the only ones in that era who heard the psalms as prophetic writings. A prophetic view of the psalms is also in one of the Dead Sea Scrolls. A scroll found there claims that David "wrote three thousand six hundred psalms....All these he uttered in prophecy, which was given him from before the Most High" (11QPs, column xxvii). For these Jews, the psalms were prophetic, and they bore an important message for those who interpreted them correctly.

As early Christians continued praying the psalms, many of the words and images made much more sense to them as they remembered Jesus: They began to realize that in the psalms there were hints that Jesus was the Messiah (for example, Acts 18:28). Their preachers told the story of Jesus' passion and death, haunted by the words of certain psalms, especially psalms of innocent sufferers. For them, Jesus was the premier innocent sufferer. Not surprisingly, the writers of the stories of Jesus' passion, death, and resurrection seem to have been inspired by some of the details in Psalms 22, 31, and 69, which are amply quoted in the various passion narratives. Proclaiming the death and resurrection of Jesus in a worship context that probably also included readings from Jewish scriptures was an ideal setting for showing him as messiah and fulfillment of those prophecies in their scriptures. Matthew, Mark, and Luke cite liberally from the psalms in their passion narratives. The following list presents some of the psalm verses used in the passion narratives; you may find the exact location in the notes of your own bibles. The psalm citations appear in italics.

Mark, often considered the earliest of the gospels, cites many psalm verses in chapter 15.

23 *And they offered him wine mixed with myrrh* (Ps 69:22); but he did not take it.

24 And they crucified him, and *divided his clothes*

among them, casting lots to decide what each should take. (Ps 22:19)

29 *Those who passed by derided him, shaking their heads and saying, "Aha!* (Ps 22:8) You who would destroy the temple and build it in three days,

30 save yourself, and come down from the cross!"

31 In the same way the chief priests, along with the scribes, were also *mocking him among themselves and saying, "He saved others; he cannot save himself."* (Ps 22:9)

34 At three o'clock Jesus cried out with a loud voice, *"Eloi, Eloi, lema sabachthani?" which means, "My God, my God, why have you forsaken me?"* (Ps 22:2)

36 *And someone ran, filled a sponge with sour wine, put it on a stick, and gave it to him to drink.* (Ps 69:22)

Matthew 27 contains the same citations, and adds one: *"He trusts in God; let God deliver him now, if he wants to"* (Ps 22:9; Matt 27:43).

Finally, Luke 23 presents most of the same citations as Mark and Matthew, but adds an important one, "Then Jesus, crying with a loud voice, said, 'Father, into your hands I commend my spirit'" (Ps 31:6; Luke 23:46).

Although three psalms significantly influenced the writing of the story of Jesus' passion and death, Psalm 22 clearly stands out as most important. Mark and Matthew recall Jesus' dying words on the cross as, "My God, my God, why have you abandoned me," the opening verse of Psalm 22. We can imagine that Jesus knew the whole psalm and often prayed it by heart; now, at the moment of his agony, he cries out to God in words he has so often prayed during his life. Two gospel accounts reflect Jesus praying words from Psalm 22 as he died, so it seems natural that early Christians would have meditated often on this psalm in their prayer and worship. As the evangelists composed accounts of Jesus' passion, certain verses and images from this psalm may have jogged their memories and also helped them to organize the way that they would recount the events for their communities. If Jesus knew the psalms well, so did his disciples and their followers.

These three psalms have something important in common: Each echoes the voice of an innocent person suffering cruel opposition and persecution. They are psalms of the suffering just ones and take the form of lament psalms. Jesus had preeminent cause to call out to God, his Father, for saving help in face of such cruelty. As many have expressed it, when a Christian prays a lament psalm it is not difficult to pray it with the suffering Jesus. This particular group of lament psalms became the religious language with which early Christians interpreted and retold the passion of Jesus. For the evangelists, then, Psalms 22, 31, and 69 offered images of unjustified suffering that deepened the spiritual dimension of their account of Christ's passion and death. In particular, Psalms 22 and 31 have become psalms in which the innocent and suffering Jesus addresses God, showing how in some of the psalms Christ is praying to his Father.

ROYAL, MESSIANIC PSALMS

Early Christians searched the psalms to find other ways to "speak about" Jesus. As they came to recognize him as the Messiah of Israel, the "anointed one," like Israel's kings, they also began to hear the Jewish messianic psalms as prophecies of Christ. Most of these psalms originated as royal psalms, used in ancient Israel in connection with the Davidic king, from the world of the ancient monarchy of Israel. The common element in all of them is the way they relate to different aspects of the king's life. The king was understood to rule as God's representative on earth, and spoke to people in that role; he also represented the people before God as a type of intermediary. In the Ancient Near East, especially in Egypt, kings were usually considered divine, sons of god. In Israel, some psalms speak of the king as "son of God" to indicate the king's close relationship with God, even though he remained human. Davidic kings ruled over people, and God guaranteed the king's rule and kingdom. They also played an important role in Israel's worship, so many psalms relate to public festivities in Israel in which the king was central. Several psalms celebrate the king's coronation or anniversary: Psalms 2, 21, 72, 101, and 110. Psalm 45 seems to preserve a royal wedding song. Psalm 20 recounts a king's prayer for victory in battle, while Psalm 18 articulates a royal thanksgiving song after God granted victory. A list of royal psalms includes at least the following: Psalms 2, 18, 20, 21, 45, 72, 89, 101, 110, 132, and 144:1–11.

As the early Christians pondered such psalms, they identified them with the reign of God, which they gradually envisioned as Jesus' rule over all creation. In a special way three royal psalms became messianic psalms related to Jesus: Psalms 2, 72, and 110. In Psalms 2 and 110 the relationship of Jesus as Son of God was easily perceived in the "son of God" language applied to Jesus. Early Christians pondered these psalms and understood Jesus Christ's life and mission better through them, and some writers included them in their letters to other Christians. When they prayed these psalms, they inevitably made connections with Christ and spoke of them as messianic.

Hearing psalms in the liturgy, in the context of people worshiping God with Christ, led to more and more connections with Christ even in other psalms that had never been considered royal or messianic.

PSALMS AS PROPHETIC IN LATER CHRISTIAN WRITINGS

So Christians began with a group of messianic psalms, which contained nearly explicit allusions to Christ, and gradually developed the idea that the entire psalter is christological (Brook 1992, 83). Remember that the fathers of the church, indeed most early Christians, encountered the psalms in public worship, where their context was explicitly Christ-centered. They understood themselves as worshiping God in Christ, through Christ, and with Christ. Most houses of worship constructed after the time of Constantine contained visual and spatial hints that all their prayer and worship was "in Christ." Many churches featured the cross, whether in a representation or in the shaping of the church space, while many Byzantine churches featured icons of Christ, often of Christ Pantocrator hovering over the central dome of the church. Many teachings of the fathers of the church began as sermons at worship or were oriented to worship rather than to the classroom or academy. The Christ-centered approach to the psalms grew out of holistic experience of the psalms, experienced in various sounds, sights, and smells, gestures and movements, and feelings, with proclamation, singing, and prayers directed to God with Christ. As Mary Collins puts it, "Christological insight arises not from psalms studied exegetically and interpreted doctrinally or dogmatically, but from psalms sung in the heart of the Spirit-filled Church and from the preaching of pastors grounded in such ecclesial prayer" (Collins 1996, 73).

By the third and fourth centuries Christians tended to consider the psalms as "prayers addressed *to* Christ who is the Yahweh of the psalms; from A.D. 400 into the Middle Ages...the psalms were prayers *of* Christ, whose mystical body embraced all men and women" (Stuhlmueller 1983a, 49). Historians usually credit Augustine with this shift, understanding the psalms as Christ's prayer in which we can and should join our own voices. His later sermons and commentaries on the psalms point in this direction. Mary Clark interprets him:

> Jesus Christ, who on earth prayed the psalms, now prays them with his members. He won these members by his life and death on the cross (EnP 138:12). With us, therefore, as we pray the psalms, he offers to the Father praise, gratitude, sorrow for our sins, petitions for grace. In some psalms Christ alone speaks as invisible Head of the Church (Ps 91:14–16; 34:12–23). At other times the "total Christ" speaks—Head and members....Sometimes the voice of the Church alone can be heard (EnP 5:1). (Clark 1996, 92)

When we pray psalms, we may use Augustine's approach and ask the following questions. Is Christ alone speaking in this psalm? Is the "total Christ," Christ as the church, speaking in this psalm? Or does the church alone address God in this psalm? Each question gives us a slightly different way to hear a psalm in, with, and through Christ.

In the sixteenth century Martin Luther brought the psalms to his people in the vernacular, and he taught them how to hear them as Christian prayers. In his *Preface to the Psalms* he notes that the Book of Psalms points to

Jesus Christ: "It most clearly promises the death and resurrection of Christ, and describes His kingdom, and the nature and standing of all Christian people" (quoted in Dillenberger 1961, 38). Dietrich Bonhoeffer, a German Lutheran pastor who gave his life in resistance to the Nazi regime, stands in the same tradition. In 1939–40 he wrote *The Psalms: The Prayer Book of the Bible,* his last booklet before the Nazis prohibited him from further publishing. Bonhoeffer believed that in the psalms God addressed to us the words with which we might make response, especially those prayers that Jesus uttered in his own lifetime. He puts it succinctly: "The Psalms are given to us to this end, that we may learn to pray them in the name of Jesus Christ" (Bonhoeffer 1970, 15). We can imagine what comfort and strength he gained from praying the psalms with Christ as he approached his own execution.

RESOURCES FOR CHRIST-CENTERED PRAYER WITH PSALMS

Today, some handy and helpful guides to the psalms are available, especially oriented to christological hearing and praying of psalms. We will feature three examples, one Roman Catholic, another Lutheran, and a third Presbyterian. Then we will include their particular keys to Psalms 22 and 24. You will easily recall the centrality of Psalm 22 in the passion narratives. Psalm 24, as we saw, is best described as an entry psalm, probably sung in procession to the Jerusalem Temple. Christian writers have often heard in it a hint of Christ's royal entry into our world and have composed hymnody that draws it into worship.

The Roman Catholic Liturgy of the Hours contains helpful pairs of titles given at the head of most psalms. Usually the first title describes the content of the psalm, while the second "is explicitly christological; some of these christological 'titles' are New Testament citations, while others are patristic" (Collins 1996, 74). For Psalm 22, the two headings are "God hears the suffering of his Holy One" and Matthew 27:46: "Jesus cried out with a loud voice: My God, my God, why have you forsaken me?" The first title allows one to identify the situation, and the second explicitly links it with Christ's life. For Psalm 24, the two headings are "The Lord's entry into his temple" and "Christ opened the door for us in the manhood he assumed" (St. Irenaeus). This early father of the church connects this entry psalm with the incarnation, the entry of God into the world as human.

A recent Lutheran publication, *Psalms with Introductions by Martin Luther,* provides a rich source of Luther's christological understanding of the psalms (Cameron 1993). In Psalms 22 and 24 Luther sees prophecies of events in Christ's life (Ps 22) and of the kingdom of Christ come into the world (Ps 24).

> The 22nd psalm is a prophecy of the suffering and resurrection of Christ and of the Gospel, which the entire world shall hear and receive. Beyond all other texts, it clearly shows Christ's torments on the cross, that he was pierced hand and foot and his limbs stretched out so that his bones could have been counted....It is indeed one of the chief psalms. (Cameron 1993, 30)

> The 24th psalm is a prophecy of the coming worldwide kingdom of Christ. It calls on the "doors" of the world, that is, the kings and princes, to make way for the kingdom of Christ. They and those who for the most part rage against him (Ps 2) say, "Who

> is this king of glory?...Shall he be a king and shall we
> yield and submit to him? We shall not!" In this way
> the psalm shows that God's Word will certainly be
> condemned and persecuted. (Cameron 1993, 33)

Luther's words on Psalm 24 invite us to formulate our response to this king, to God incarnate.

The recent Presbyterian *Book of Common Worship* contains 127 psalms suggested for various services of corporate worship. Accompanying each is a psalm prayer that "captures some theme or image from the psalm and often addresses Christian implications drawn from the psalm. The prayer helps us to pray the psalm and to see Christ in the psalm as we pray" (*Book of Common Worship* 1993, 600). Again, the prayers composed for Psalm 22 and Psalm 24 are very good examples of this approach.

> *Psalm 22:* Eternal God, your tortured Son felt abandoned, and cried out in anguish from the cross, yet you delivered him. He overcame the bonds of death and rose in triumph from the grave. Do not hide your face from those who cry out to you. Feed the hungry, strengthen the weak, and break the chains of the oppressed, that your people may rejoice in your saving deeds. (*Book of Common Worship* 1993, 634)
>
> *Psalm 24:* God of all creation, open our hearts that Christ, the King of glory, may enter and rule over our lives. Give us clean hands and pure hearts, that we may stand in your presence and receive your blessing through the same Jesus Christ our Lord. (*Book of Common Worship* 1993, 636)

Any of these three resources can help us read, hear, or pray these psalms in, through, and with Jesus Christ.

RESPONSORIAL PSALMS IN THE LECTIONARY

In the revised liturgical texts of many churches a responsorial psalm comes between two of the scripture lessons. In many cases a psalm was chosen because either the first reading or the gospel text cited or alluded to a psalm or seemed to have a literary connection to a psalm. For example, on the Third Sunday of Easter, Good Shepherd Sunday, Psalm 23 is used. But for the important seasons of the church year Christians traditionally singled out particular psalms, and these often appear in the revised Roman lectionary (Deiss 1996, 106–7).

Advent: Psalms 25, 80, 85   Holy Week: Psalm 22

Christmas week: Psalms 96, 97, 98   Easter season: Psalms 66, 118

Epiphany cycle: Psalm 72   Pentecost: Psalm 104

Lent: Psalms 26, 51, 91, 130

You might enjoy praying these psalms during their appropriate seasons or whenever you wish to pray or meditate on these events or mysteries of Christ's life.

LORD: AN AFRICAN AMERICAN SAVING JESUS

Lament-like songs and psalms have played a most important role in the spirituals of the African American

228 ● A RETREAT WITH THE PSALMS

church. These songs of pain, longing, and hope also focused on trust in Jesus. We recently heard a moving recording of a concert by Aretha Franklin in which a beautiful spiritual surrounded her reading of Psalm 23. She focuses on Jesus as her personal shepherd, and names him as Lord. Addressing God as Lord or hearing about the Lord often brings up images of a saving Lord in this worshiping community. This deep sensitivity emerged in discussions about how to translate YHWH/Adonay in the psalms for a recent Roman Catholic translation. Because many people feel that naming God as Lord is too gender-specific (an exclusively male-oriented word), the translators considered alternatives. The commission, however, included members from many different countries and cultures, some of whom expressed far less concern about using the word *Lord*, because it "gets more varied use" in their cultures (for example, "Lord Mayor" is used for women as well as men in Scotland, England, and Ireland). But they also knew of discussions in North America, when the National Council of Churches was working on its inclusive-language lectionary. Many African Americans objected to a proposal to eliminate the word *Lord* from this translation because of their own social history: "Oppression and oppressors they knew well enough, but the oppressor that endured had not been the one they called 'Lord.' While lording it over others was white people's sin, 'Lord Jesus' and 'King Jesus' had kept black people's hopes alive" (Collins 1996, xxxix). For them, the Lordship of Jesus is a saving and liberating reality in their lives, especially in the context of the racism of white Christians in the United States. To give up this term of address to Christ would be tantamount to losing memory of the salvation from oppression that they had experienced in Jesus. This vignette demonstrates the powerfully liberating potential of praying to Jesus and to God as saving Lord.

PRAYING PSALMS IN, WITH, AND THROUGH CHRIST

As we pray with these psalms, we can allow them to reveal to us the very interior passages and entryways of Christ's own self. Moving slowly with these psalms we can feel fear and sorrow with Jesus, call out to God and profess trust along with him, try to hear in these psalms the multiple experiences and feelings and emotions that Jesus himself felt in his lifetime. We might also beg the Spirit to open our eyes to the total Christ, the Christ of the entire Christian church—through all the earth, through all the ages—and its hopes and fears, sorrows and joys, laments and praises. As some have put it, with the psalms we pass through the heart and soul and mind of Christ, joining ourselves to his own experience through our prayer with psalms.

PSALMS THROUGHOUT THE WEEK

● Jesus, as an observant Jew of his time, would have prayed the succession of psalms for the days of the week and for Sabbath. In union with Jesus Christ, each day of the week pray the following psalms: Sunday (Ps 24), Monday (Ps 48), Tuesday (Ps 82), Wednesday (Pss 94 and Ps 95:1), Thursday (Ps 81), Friday morning (Ps 93), Friday evening, beginning of Sabbath (Pss 29 and 95—99), Saturday morning (Ps 92, "a Sabbath song"), Saturday evening, blessing to begin the new week (Ps 91).
● After praying this sequence for several weeks, reflect: What have I experienced about sanctifying time? What have I learned about Jesus? What have I experienced as I joined in the sequence he probably prayed?

PRAYING WITH CHRIST THROUGH HOLY WEEK

• Use your imagination to go on a spiritual pilgrimage with Jesus through the events of Holy Week. You may wish to follow the format of *lectio divina*.

Palm Sunday:
Pss 24 and 118
 (especially vv. 25–26)

Holy Thursday:
Pss 23, 34
Pss 113, 114 (before Seder)
Pss 115, 116, 117, 118
 (after Seder)
Ps 136

Good Friday:
Pss 22, 31, 69. Lamentations

Easter:
Ps 118 (especially vv. 22–24)

JOINING WITH THE SUFFERING CHRIST

• As we pray Psalm 22 on Good Friday, we need only to focus on Jesus' cry to God from the cross, pleading with God not to abandon him: "My God, my God, why have you forsaken me?" What may sound like a cry of desperation on the lips of another cannot be that—not because it is Jesus who cries out, but because he pours out the words of this psalm of lament, which includes within it the seeds of hope and trust in God: "In you our ancestors trusted; they trusted and you rescued them" (v. 5, RNAB). He prayed this psalm now as never before. With Jesus, we can enter into the pain and the hope, gradually joining our own pain and hope to his, as well as that of all suffering ones in the church and world today.
• Pray Psalm 22 in the style of *lectio divina*. Or you may choose another of the psalms that appears in the passion narratives in the gospels or in the liturgical texts of Holy Week.

1. As you begin, ask for the grace to enter into the suffering of Christ and to understand and appropriate its meaning for you, or for us, today. Notice, for example, that in the second part of the psalm (vv. 22–31), the speaker shifts to thankful praise of God. Can you imagine this change in Christ's prayer? Has it ever been your experience?

2. Allow the movements of *lectio divina* to flow in and out for as long as they are lively, or for as long as you have set aside for prayer.

3. At the conclusion of this time, note in your journal the words or phrases you selected for attention, some of the ruminations or insights that came to you, particularly about Jesus and about yourself in relation to his passion. How did you feel inclined to respond to God as you contemplated the suffering of Jesus through the words of the psalm?

PRAYING THE PSALMS WITH IGNATIUS LOYOLA

• Some people have made a practice of praying with psalm texts while making the *Spiritual Exercises* of St. Ignatius. This spiritual teacher, who referred to himself as the Pilgrim in his autobiography, can offer us a way to make a spiritual pilgrimage in our hearts and minds, in contemplative prayer. Even if we never visit the sites that invite pilgrimage, we may journey to them in the prayer exercises Ignatius suggests, in the Second Week (the incarnation and ministry of Christ), the Third Week (Christ's passion and death), and the Fourth Week (Christ's resurrection). Some people have found much profit in praying a psalm, or part of a psalm, as an introduction to a time of prayer on a particular scene in Christ's life. Others conclude a time of prayer by praying such a psalm text with Jesus, who may have prayed in this fashion. You will find two sets of suggested psalm texts in Appendix 2.

PRAYING HANDEL'S *MESSIAH*

• Contemplatively listen to a recording of Handel's *Messiah,* especially Part II (#27–43, in particular), in which he adapts parts of Psalms 2, 16, 22, 24, 68, and 69 into his text. Approach it not as a performance but as a prayer. Appendix 3 gives more background on the *Messiah* and contains a chart that identifies the psalm references. Notice the way Handel employs psalms to interpret the mystery of his subject. How do you feel moved to respond to God in light of Handel's music?

SINGING CHRISTOLOGICAL INTERPRETATIONS OF THE PSALMS

• Embedded deeply within certain hymn-singing traditions are christological interpretations of the psalms. Select one or several of the following Christianized psalms. Sing it several times, letting it settle within you. Let the psalm idiom teach you the cadence of Christian prayer as it did our forebears. Following your singing of the hymn, read the psalm contemplatively, then conclude with the hymn.

Psalm	Title	Tune/Composer	Hymnal
22	My God, My God	Manion	G&P
22	In the Presence of Your People	The Celebration Song	WOV
23	The King of Love, My Shepherd Is	St. Columba	most hymnals
23	My Shepherd Will Supply My Need	Resignation CMD	PH, W, HEC
24	Lift Up Your Heads, You Mighty Gate	Truro LM	PH, UMH, NCH
24	All Glory, Laud, and Honor	St. Theodulph	W

24	The King of Glory	Gilu Hagalim	most hymnals
72	Hail to the Lord's Anointed	Ellacombe	W, G
72	To Jesus Christ Our Sovereign King	Ich Glaub' An Gott	UMH, NCH
72	Crown Him with Many Crowns	Diademata SMD	W, G, G&P
72	Jesus Shall Reign	Duke Street LM	W, G, G&P
98	Joy to the World	Antioch CM	W, LBW
98	All the Ends of the Earth	Dufford	most hymnals
117	From All That Dwell Below the Skies	Old Hundredth, Lasst Uns Erfreuen, Duke Street	G&P most hymnals
118	This Is the Day	Gelineau	G

• In your post-prayer reflections, note your responses to the following: How does this psalm speak of Jesus Christ for the hymn writer? Does it to speak to you of any other aspects of Christ's life, or of your relationship with Christ? How does prayerful singing of this hymn build faith in Christ present in the community?

COMMUNAL EVENING PRAYER:
CHRIST AND THE PSALMS

Pray the following prayer in common, if possible. Use your community's hymnal to select appropriate hymns, antiphons, and psalms for singing. The opening sentences, psalm prayer, and dismissal are adapted from *Daily Prayer* 1987, 59, 213, 240, and 76.

Service of Light
> Light and peace in Jesus Christ our Lord. **Thanks be to God.**
> Let us give thanks to the God of our Lord Jesus Christ. **God has blessed us in Christ with every spiritual blessing.**
> Before the world was made, God chose us in Christ, **that we might be holy and blameless before God.**
> (Eph 1:3–4)

Evening Hymn: "Phos Hilaron" or another evening hymn

Psalm 22 (sung or recited antiphonally)

Psalm Prayer
> Eternal God, when your Son accepted the cross and felt abandoned by you, he cried out to you. Then death was destroyed, and life was restored. By his death and resurrection, liberate the poor, lift up the downtrodden, break the chains of the oppressed, that your church may sing your praises. **Amen.**

Psalm 118 (sung or recited antiphonally/responsorially)

Psalm Prayer
> O God, your Son, rejected by the builders, has become the cornerstone of the church. Shed rays of your glory throughout the earth that all may shout with joy in celebration of the wonder of Christ's resurrection, now and forever. **Amen.**

Reading: Ephesians 2:19–22

Silent Reflection (or brief homily)

Gospel Canticle: Canticle of Mary (sung or recited antiphonally)

Litany of the Holy Name

Left: Lord, have mercy.

Right: Lord, have mercy.

L: Christ, have mercy.

R: Christ, have mercy.

L: Lord, have mercy.

R: Lord, have mercy.

L: God our Father in heaven.

R: Have mercy on us.

L: Lord, be merciful.

R: Jesus, save your people.

L: Christ, hear us.

R. Christ, hear us.

L: Lord Jesus, hear our prayer.

R: Lord Jesus, hear our prayer.

The Lord's Prayer

Concluding Prayers

May God's peace, which is far beyond our understanding, keep us safe in union with Christ Jesus. **Amen.**

Bless the Lord. **The Lord's name be praised.**

Appendix 1
Psalms by Types

The list below represents our best estimate of types in the psalter, but remember that other opinions may be found, since types or genre classifications of psalms are not an exact science. Moreover, some psalms may be classified in two distinct ways, for example, a royal lament (Ps 69) or a penitential psalm of thanksgiving (Ps 32). Some psalms appear in two different lists; these are marked with an asterisk (*) each time they appear.

Laments
> Of an individual: 3, 4, 5, 6*, 7, 9—10*, 13, 14, 17, 22, 25, 26, 27*, 28, 31, 35, 38*, 39, 40*, 41*, 42, 43, 51*, 52, 53, 54, 55, 56, 57, 59, 61*, 64, 69, 70, 71, 86, 88, 102*, 109, 120, 130*, 139*, 140, 141, 142, 143*
> Of the community: 12, 44, 58, 60, 74, 77, 79, 80, 83, 85, 89*, 90, 94, 123, 126, 137

Thanksgiving
> Of an individual: 9—10*, 18*, 30, 32*, 34*, 40*, 41*, 92*, 116, 138
> Of the community: 65, 66*, 67, 75, 107, 118, 124, 129

Songs of Trust and Confidence
11, 16, 23, 27*, 62, 63, 91, 108, 115*, 121, 125, 131

Praise (Hymns)
8, 19*, 24*, 29, 33, 47*, 66*, 92*, 93*, 95—100*, 103, 104, 111, 113, 114, 115*, 117, 135*, 136*, 145—150.
Focus on God as creator: 8*, 19*, 29*, 33*, 104*
Of the enthronement of God: 47*, 93*, 95—100*

Songs of Zion (Jerusalem)
46, 48, 76, 84, 87, 122

Royal Psalms
2, 18*, 20, 21, 45, 61*, 72, 89*, 101, 110, 144

Wisdom Psalms
1*, 34*, 36, 37, 49, 73, 76, 112, 119*, 127, 128, 133, 139*

Liturgical Psalms (associated with covenant)
15, 24*, 50, 68, 81, 82, 132, 134

Torah Psalms
1*, 19*, 119*

Penitential Psalms
6*, 32*, 38*, 51*, 102*, 130*, 143*

Appendix 2
Praying Psalms with the *Spiritual Exercises*

Juan Benitez (1965) suggests the following psalms to accompany the *Spiritual Exercises:*

Introduction: Ps 139

Principal and Foundation
God: Ps 90:1–11
God, Creator of the universe: Pss 19:1–7; 104:1–25, 29
God, Creator of humans: Ps 139:9–10, 13–16
Presence of God: Ps 139:1–8
Destiny of humans: Ps 39:2–8

First Week
History of sin: Ps 25:6–22
Sins of humans: Ps 58
Our own sins: Pss 51:3–7, 11–14; 38:2–19
First colloquy on sins: [*Spiritual Exercises* #53]
    "What have I done for Christ?" Ps 51:1–13
    "What am I doing for Christ?" Ps 26:2
    "What ought I to do for Christ?" Ps 26:3–12
    To beg for the light: "What ought I to do for Christ?"
    Ps 27:11–14

Second colloquy (*Spiritual Exercises* #61)
 Gratitude: Ps 65:1–9
 Petition: Ps 80:8–16
 Amendment: Ps 80:18–20
Triple colloquy (*Spiritual Exercises* #63)
 1. "A deep knowledge of my sins and a feeling of abhorrence for them." Ps 19:10–15
 2. "An understanding of the disorder of my actions, that filled with horror of them, I may amend my life and put it in order." Pss 50:16–22; 52:3–6
 3. "A knowledge of the world." Ps 25:6–18
Hell: Pss 37:9–10; 38; 52:7–9; 58:7–12
Torment of the condemned: Pss 83:12–19; 38:6–12
Colloquy on hell: Pss 6:1–8; 130
Death: Pss 103:14–16; 90:3–6, 10–12; 102:25, 28; 55:24; 139:16–18
Repentance and gratitude: Pss 85; 103:1–10; 32:1–7
The justice of God: Pss 50:4–7; 59:6
Joy in God's justice: Ps 67:1–5
God, judge of the wicked: Ps 94:1–4, 9–11
Joy of the just over God's fairness: Ps 96:9–13

Second Week
Temporal King
 1. Royal figure: Ps 45:1–8
 2. Security of those who follow him: Ps 46:1–4
Qualities of the King
 1. Justice: Ps 72:1–7
 2. Mercy: Ps 72:13–16
 3. Dominion and Power: Ps 72:8–12
 4. Holiness: Ps 72:17–19
Jesus Christ: his power: Ps 110:1–3
Jesus Christ: eternal priest: Ps 110:4–7
Birth of Jesus: Pss 40:7–9; 2:7–10
"Who is the child of God?" Pss 8:4–7; 24:8–10; 45:3
The power of the infant God: Ps 72:8–13

Joy over the coming of Jesus: Pss 117; 118:1–6
Presentation of Jesus in the Temple: Pss 84:3–11; 40:7–9
The hidden life: Nazareth, obedience: Ps 119:9–16
Love of the Law: Ps 119:25–32, 45–48
The [Two] Standards:
    Petition: Ps 143:8–10
    How Satan proceeds: Ps 59:7–8, 13–16
    God frees us from the evil leader: Ps 3:1–7
    The Law of God: Ps 19:8–12
    The life-giving life of Jesus: Ps 119:29–36
    The army of the good leader: Ps 34:4–9
Prayer and teaching of Jesus Christ: Pss 62:1–8; 63:1–5
The temptations: Pss 86:1–8, 14–16; 63:7–10
Triumph over the temptations: Ps 91:2–7, 14–16
Call of the rich young man: Pss 52:7–9; 49:1–10
Expulsion of the merchants from the temple: Ps 79:1, 5–7

Third Week
The Last Supper: Ps 23
Thanks for all benefits: Ps 136:1–2, 5, 23–26
Exit of Judas: Ps 41:10
Prayer in the Garden: Pss 69:1–10; 31:10–11
Arrest of Jesus: Pss 54:4–5; 62:4–5
Kiss of Judas: Ps 55:13–15
Crowning with thorns: Pss 69:8–13; 41:7–8; 55:18–21
In the Sanhedrin: Pss 56:7; 64:2–7; 58:2–6
The scourging: Ps 38:6–13
Carrying the cross: Ps 70:2–4; 31:11–14
The crucifixion: Pss 42:10–12; 22:2–4, 7–9, 14–19; 88:2–10, 19
"I am thirsty": Ps 69:22
Burial of Jesus: Pss 16:1–2, 9–11; Ps 4

Fourth Week
Resurrection of Jesus Christ: Pss 3:4–6; 116:7–8; 57:8–9; 47:2–9

Jesus' station in heaven: Ps 16:8–11
The Father's reward to Jesus: Pss 21:2–7; 45:2–8
Appearance to the apostles:
1. Joy: Ps 145:1, 12–15, 20–21
2. Union and love: Ps 133
The Ascension: Pss 24:7–10; 47:6–10

Contemplation for Obtaining Love
"Because it is good": Pss 136:1, 5–9; 24:1–2; 104:24–28
Cosmic praise to God: Ps 148
Final symphony: Ps 150

In a more general treatment of the movements of the
Spiritual Exercises, Luis Alonso-Schökel (1996) offers
these psalm suggestions:

Principle and Foundation
Psalms 8, 19

Sin and Pardon
Psalms 50, 51, 130, 103

King, Call, Apostolate
King: Psalms 2, 72
Call and Response: Psalms 40, 27
Apostolic Activity: Psalms 37, 12, 82, Ezekiel 13—14

Passion
Psalms 22, 31, 55, Lamentations

Glory, Church
Glory: Psalms 20—21, 118, 57
Church: Psalms 87, 133

Union with God
Psalms 23, 16, 42—43, 131

Appendix 3
Handel's *Messiah* and the Psalms

Handel's *Messiah* has become an immensely popular musical offering in the Advent and Lent-Easter seasons. This oratorio explores New Testament themes and materials: the coming of the Messiah, his redemptive suffering (especially based on the Suffering Servant in Isaiah 53), and thanksgiving for the defeat of death in Christ's resurrection. For many, it remains a powerful spiritual reminder of a sacred season and sacred, saving events of Christ's life.

The words in the text come mostly from biblical citations that concern the life of Christ, not only from the New Testament, but also from Hebrew scripture citations long considered by many Christians as prophecies of the Christ event. This sensibility was particularly pronounced in the German Lutheran tradition from which Handel emerged. Especially prominent is the prophet Isaiah, with citations from chapters 9, 40, and 53. He also renders parts of Psalms 22, 69, 16, 24, 68, and 2.

Handel too presents many psalms long considered christological as prophecies of Christ. Several of Luther's introductions seem very appropriate. Concerning Psalm 2 (in #40–42) Luther said it prophesied "that he would suffer and through his suffering become King and Lord of the whole world" (Cameron 1993, 8). Of the defiant world powers in the psalm Luther remarks, "Within this psalm stands a warning against the world's kings and lords: if, instead of honoring and serving this king, they seek to persecute and blot him out, they shall perish" (Cameron 1993, 8). Psalm 24, rendered with Handel's memorable "Lift up Your Heads," recalls Luther's comment: "It calls on the 'doors' of the world, that is, the kings and princes, to make way for the kingdom of Christ" (Cameron 1993, 33).

Those who appreciate this oratorio as music will find great spiritual nourishment in it. In the libretto of Handel's *Messiah* you can find text according to section numbers. Below you will find sections that incorporate psalms in a christological fashion into his oratorio.

Section #	Psalm	Handel's text
27–28	Ps 22:7–8	"All they that see Him, laugh him to scorn" and "He trusted in God that He would deliver him"—Christ's suffering.
29	Ps 69:20	"Thy rebuke has broken His heart"—Christ's suffering.
32	Ps 16:10	"But thou didst not leave His soul in hell [psalm reads 'my soul'], nor didst Thou suffer Thy Holy One to see corruption"—prophecy of Christ's victory over death.
33	Ps 24:7–10	"'Lift up your heads, O ye gates'; and be ye lift up, ye everlasting doors; and the King of glory shall come in. Who is the King of glory? The Lord strong and mighty, the Lord mighty in battle. Lift up your heads, O ye gates; and be ye lift up, ye everlasting doors; and the King of glory shall come in.

Who is the King of glory? The Lord of Hosts, He is the King of glory."

36	Ps 68:18	"Thou art gone up on high, Thou hast led captivity captive, and received gifts for men; yea, even for Thine enemies, that the Lord God may dwell among them"—Christ ascended to heaven.
37	Ps 68:11	"The Lord gave the word; great was the company of preachers"—dissemination of the gospel.
40–43	Ps 2:1–4, 9	"Why do the nations so furiously rage together? [and] why do the people imagine a vain thing? The kings of the earth rise up, and the rulers take counsel together against the Lord, and against His Anointed."

"Let us break their bonds asunder, and cast away their yokes from us."

"He that dwelleth in heaven shall laugh them to scorn; the Lord shall have them in derision."

"Thou shalt break them with a rod of iron; Thou shalt dash them in pieces like a potter's vessel"—continued human defiance of the gospel.

BIBLIOGRAPHY

WORKS ON THE PSALMS AND THE BIBLE

Alonso-Schökel, Luis. 1988. *A Manual of Hebrew Poetics*. Rome: Pontificio Istituto Biblico.

————. 1996a. *Contempladlo y Quedaréis Radiantes: Salmos y Ejercicios*. Santander: Editorial Sal Terrae.

————. 1996b. "True Language of the Human Spirit: The Language of the Psalms." *The Way Supplement* 87 (Autumn).

Anderson, Bernhard W., with Steven Bishop. 2000. *Out of the Depths: The Psalms Speak for Us Today*. Third revised and expanded edition. Louisville, Ky.: Westminster John Knox Press.

Athanasius. 1980. *Letter to Marcellinus*. In *Athanasius: The Life of Antony and the Letter to Marcellinus*. Classics of Western Spirituality. Translated and introduction by Robert C. Gregg. New York: Paulist Press.

Benitez, Juan. 1965. *Los Ejercicios Espirituales: Meditados con los Salmos*. Bilbao: El Mensajero del Corazon de Jesus.

Benson, Gaye G. 1995. "Selective Praise and Prayer—The Wesleyan Psalter Old and New." Unpublished paper, Graduate Theological Union.

Bonhoeffer, Dietrich. 1970. *Psalms: The Prayer Book of the Bible.* Minneapolis, Minn.: Augsburg Publishing House.

Brook, John. 1992. *The School of Prayer: An Introduction to the Divine Office for All Christians.* Collegeville, Minn.: The Liturgical Press.

Brueggemann, Walter. 1995. *The Psalms and the Life of Faith.* Edited by Patrick D. Miller. Minneapolis, Minn.: Augsburg Fortress.

Cameron, Bruce A. 1993. *Psalms with Introductions by Martin Luther.* St. Louis, Mo.: Concordia Publishing House.

Clark, Mary. 1996. "St. Augustine's Use of the Psalms." *The Way Supplement* 87 (Autumn).

Cohen, The Rev. Dr. A. 1945. *The Psalms: Hebrew Text, English Translation and Commentary.* Hindhead, Surrey: Soncino Press.

Collins, Mary. 1995. An Introduction to the translation. *Psalms for Morning and Evening Prayer* (ICEL Psalms), xxix–xlii. Chicago, Ill.: Liturgy Training Publications.

———. 1996. "Psalms in the Daily Office." *The Spirituality of the Psalms, The Way Supplement* 87 (Autumn).

Craghan, John. 1985. *The Psalms: Prayers for the Ups, Downs and In-Betweens of Life: A Literary-Experiential Approach.* Wilmington, Del.: Michael Glazier.

Craven, Toni. 1992. *The Book of Psalms.* A Michael Glazier Book. Collegeville, Minn.: Liturgical Press.

Davidson, Robert. 1998. *The Vitality of Worship: A Commentary on the Book of Psalms.* Grand Rapids, Mich.: William B. Eerdmans.

Drijvers, Pius. 1965. *The Psalms: Their Structure and Meaning.* Fifth revised edition. New York: Herder and Herder.

Eilberg, Rabbi Amy. 1994. "I Must Keep Singing: Introduction to Psalm 137." In *Healing of Soul, Healing of Body: Spiritual Leaders Unfold the Strength and Solace in Psalms*, edited by Rabbi Simkha Y. Weintraub, CSW, 91–95. Woodstock, Vt.: Jewish Lights Publishing.

Fritz, Maureena. 1995. *Rejoice and Be Glad: Praying With the Hebrew Scriptures*. Winona, Minn.: St. Mary's Press.

Green, Barbara. 1997. *Like a Tree Planted: An Exposition of Psalms and Parables Through Metaphor*. Collegeville, Minn.: Liturgical Press.

Gunkel, Herman. 1972. *The Psalms: A Form-Critical Introduction*. Facet Books: Biblical Series. Philadelphia: Fortress Press.

———. 1998. *Introduction to Psalms. The Genres of the Religious Lyric of Israel*. Translated by James Nogalski. Macon, Ga.: Mercer University Press, 1998. The original German edition was published in 1933.

Holladay, William. 1993. *The Psalms Through Three Thousand Years: Prayerbook of a Cloud of Witnesses*. Minneapolis, Minn.: Fortress Press.

Jinkins, Michael. 1998. *In the House of the Lord: Inhabiting the Psalms of Lament*. Collegeville, Minn.: Liturgical Press.

Kuczynski, Michael P. 1995. *Prophetic Song: The Psalms as Moral Discourse in Late Medieval England*. Philadelphia: University of Pennsylvania Press.

Levine, Herbert J. 1995. *Sing unto God a New Song: A Contemporary Reading of the Psalms*. Bloomington, Ind.: Indiana University Press.

Martini, Carlo Maria. 1992. *What Am I That You Care for Me? Praying with the Psalms*. Translated by

Dame Mary Groves, O.S.B. Collegeville, Minn.: Liturgical Press.

Merrill, Nan. 1998. *Psalms for Praying*. New York: Continuum.

Murphy, Roland. 1968. "Introduction to Wisdom Literature." In *Jerome Biblical Commentary*, edited by Raymond E. Brown, S.S., Joseph A. Fitzmyer, S.J., and Roland E. Murphy, O. Carm., 487–94. Englewood Cliffs, N.J.: Prentice-Hall.

Nowell, Irene. 1993. *Sing a New Song: The Psalms in the Sunday Lectionary*. Collegeville, Minn.: Liturgical Press.

O'Connor, Kathleen M. 1988. *The Wisdom Literature*. Wilmington, Del.: Michael Glazier.

Peterson, Eugene. 1989. *Answering God: The Psalms As Tools for Prayer*. San Francisco: Harper & Row.

Pleins, J. David. 1993. *The Psalms: Songs of Tragedy, Hope, and Justice*. Maryknoll, N.Y.: Orbis Books.

Reid, Stephen B. 1997. *Listening In: Multicultural Readings*. Nashville, Tenn.: Abingdon Press.

Prévost, Jean-Pierre. 1997. *A Short Dictionary of the Psalms*. Collegeville, Minn.: Liturgical Press.

Rienstra, Marchiene Vroon. 1992. *Swallow's Nest: A Feminine Reading of the Psalms*. Grand Rapids, Mich.: William B. Eerdmans.

Sarna, Nahum. 1993. *On the Book of Psalms: Exploring the Prayers of Ancient Israel*. New York: Schocken Books.

Stuhlmueller, Carroll. 1983a. *Psalms 1 (Psalms 1–72)*. Wilmington, Del.: Michael Glazier.

———. 1983b. *Psalms 2 (Psalms 73–150)*. Wilmington, Del.: Michael Glazier.

———. "Psalms." 1988. In *Harper's Bible Commentary*, edited by J. L. Mays, 433–94. San Francisco: Harper & Row.

Weintraub, Simkha Y., ed. 1994. *Healing of Soul, Healing of Body: Spiritual Leaders Unfold the Strength and Solace in Psalms.* Woodstock, Vt.: Jewish Lights Publishers.

Zenger, Erich. 1996. *A God of Vengeance: Understanding the Psalms of Divine Wrath.* Translated by Linda M. Maloney. Louisville, Ky.: Westminster/John Knox.

RESOURCES FOR WORSHIP AND SONG WITH PSALMS

Ambrose. 1975. "On the Psalms." *Liturgy of the Hours III.* New York: Catholic Book Publishing.

Book of Common Prayer. 1979. The Episcopal Church in the United States. New York: Church Hymnal Corporation and Seabury Press.

Book of Common Worship. 1993. Theology and Worship Ministry Unit for the Presbyterian Church (U.S.A.) and the Cumberland Presbyterian Church. Louisville, Ky.: Westminster/John Knox Press.

Brook, John. 1992. *The School of Prayer: An Introduction to the Divine Office for All Christians.* Collegeville, Minn.: Liturgical Press.

Carroll, J. Robert, ed. 1963. *The Grail/Gelineau Psalter: 150 Psalms and 18 Canticles.* Chicago: GIA Publications.

Christian Prayer: The Liturgy of the Hours. 1976. New York: Catholic Book Publishing Co.

Daily Prayer: The Worship of God. 1987. Supplemental Liturgical Resource 5. Office of Worship for the Presbyterian Church (U.S.A.) and the Cumberland Presbyterian Church. Philadelphia: The Westminster Press.

Deiss, Lucien, C.S.Sp. 1996. *Visions of Liturgy and Music for a New Century*. Collegeville, Minn.: The Liturgical Press.

Dillenberger, John. 1961. *Martin Luther: Selections from His Writings*. Edited with an introduction. Garden City, N.Y.: Anchor Books, Doubleday & Company.

———. 1975. *John Calvin: Selections from His Writings*. Edited with an introduction. Missoula, Mont.: Scholars Press.

Dreitcer, Andrew Deeter. 1997. "Lectio Divina for Groups." Unpublished class handout. San Francisco Theological Seminary, Certificate in the Art of Spiritual Direction.

Gather: Comprehensive. 1994. Chicago: GIA Publications.

Glory and Praise. 1997. Second edition. Portland, Oreg.: Oregon Catholic Press.

Guimont, Michel. 1998. *Lectionary Psalms*. Chicago: GIA Publications.

Haas, David. 1998. *Psalms for the Church Year*. Vol. 9 (CD-430). Chicago: GIA Publications.

Haïk-Vantoura, Suzanne. n.d. *La musique de la Bible révélée*. Harmonia Mundi France, cassette (HMA 43989) CD (HMA 190989); Volume 2: Paris: Erato/Fondation Roi David, cassette (FRD 803–B); Volume 3: Paris: Fondation Roi David, cassette (FRD 803–C).

Henderson, J. Frank. 1994. *Liturgies of Lament*. Chicago: Liturgy Training Publications.

Hymnal 1982. New York: Church Hymnal Corporation.

ICEL (International Commission on English in the Liturgy). 1994. *The Psalter*. Chicago: Liturgy Training Publications.

———. 1995. *Psalms for Morning and Evening Prayer*. Chicago: Liturgy Training Publications.

An Inclusive-Language Psalter of the Christian People. 1993. Collegeville, Minn.: Liturgical Press.

Kushner, Harold S. 1989. *When Bad Things Happen to Good People.* New York: Schocken Books.

Lang, Jovian, O.F.M. 1989. *Dictionary of the Liturgy.* New York: Catholic Book Publishing Co.

Larsen, Jens Peter. 1957. *Handel's* Messiah: *Origins, Compositions, Sources.* New York: W. W. Norton & Company.

The Liturgy of the Hours. 1975. Four volumes. New York: Catholic Book Publishing Company.

Lutheran Book of Worship. 1978. Ministers Desk edition. Minneapolis: Augsburg; Philadelphia: Board of Publication, Lutheran Church in America.

Milgrom, Jo. 1992. *Handmade Midrash.* Philadelphia: Jewish Publication Society.

New Century Hymnal. 1995. Cleveland, Ohio: The Pilgrim Press.

New Lectionary Psalms: Grail/Gelineau. 1998. Chicago: GIA Publications.

The New Revised Standard Version Bible: Catholic Edition. 1993. Nashville, Tenn.: Catholic Bible Press, a division of Thomas Nelson, Inc.

Norris, Kathleen. 1996. *The Cloister Walk.* New York: Riverhead Books.

Paul VI. 1975. "Introduction." *Liturgy of the Hours I.* New York: Catholic Book Publishing.

The Presbyterian Hymnal: Hymns, Psalms, and Spiritual Songs. 1990. Louisville, Ky.: Westminster/John Knox.

The Psalms of the New American Bible. 1991. Revised edition. New York: Catholic Book Publishing Co.

The Psalter: Psalms and Canticles for Singing. 1993. Louisville, Ky.: Westminster/John Knox.

Ramsay, Nancy J. 1998. "Compassionate Resistance: An Ethic for Pastoral Care and Counseling." *Journal of Pastoral Care* 52 (Fall 1998), 217–26.

Rilke, Rainer Maria. 1949. *Rilke: Selected Poems.* Translated by C. F. MacIntyre. Berkeley, Calif.: University of California Press.

Singing the Psalms. n.d. Vols. 1 (CD 10643GC), 2 (CD 10644GC), 3 (10645GC), 4 (10608GC). Portland: Oregon Catholic Press.

Starret, Martha, O.P. 1998. "Music and Dance as Response to Psalms." Transcript of a talk given in July at Bon Secours Spirituality Center, Marriottsville, Md.

United Methodist Hymnal. 1989. Nashville, Tenn.: United Methodist Publishing House.

Werner, Eric. 1960. *The Sacred Bridge: The Interdependence of Liturgy and Music in Synagogue and Church During the First Millennium.* New York: Columbia University Press.

Winton-Henry, Cynthia. 1985. *Leaps of Faith: Improvisational Dance in Worship and Education.* Austin, Tex.: The Sharing Company.

———. 1989. *The Power of Dance: Its Attraction and Threat.* Oakland, Calif.: WING IT! Press.

With One Voice: A Lutheran Resource for Worship. 1995. Minneapolis: Augsburg.

Wolff, Pierre. 1979. *May I Hate God?* New York: Paulist Press.

Worship: A Hymnal and Service Book for Roman Catholics. 1986. Third edition. Chicago: GIA Publications.

ON-LINE RESOURCES

For an online index of psalms settings and hymns inspired by psalms (from nine current church hymnals), please consult:

www.joshua.sfts.edu/liebert

For additional materials on psalms and spirituality, please consult:

http://www.jstb.edu/jendres